Trash TO TREASURE

You may not realize it, but your garbage cans and recycle bins hold almost everything you need to fashion dozens of exciting and inventive treasures! This fun new volume of Trash to Treasure *will introduce you to a multitude of unique crafts, all created using items you might ordinarily throw away. You don't have to be an experienced crafter or spend lots of money to transform things once considered useless clutter into magnificent works of "recycled" art! Browse through the four crafty sections filled with fresh ways to breathe new life into old throwaways. Our Garden Inspirations will open your eyes to novel ideas for the garden or patio, and Decorative Touches offers a bundle of ways to spruce up your home's interior. Get the entire family involved with the variety of resourceful ideas included in Fun Fix-ups. Add life to any special occasion with projects from Creative Celebrations. With our easy-to-follow instructions and full-color photographs, you'll be on your way to clever "recycling" in no time. So start turning the pages of this imaginative book, and begin looking at "trash" in a whole new way!*

LEISURE ARTS, INC.
Little Rock, AR

EDITORIAL STAFF

Vice President and Editor-in-Chief: Sandra Graham Case
Executive Director of Publications: Cheryl Nodine Gunnells
Director of Designer Relations: Debra Nettles
Design Director: Cyndi Hansen
Editorial Director: Susan Frantz Wiles
Publications Director: Kristine Anderson Mertes
Photography Director: Lori Ringwood Dimond
Art Operations Director: Jeff Curtis

DESIGN
Lead Designer: Diana Sanders Cates
Senior Designers: Polly Tullis Browning, Peggy Cunningham, and Anne Pulliam Stocks
Designers: Cherece Athy, Linda Diehl Tiano, and Becky Werle
Craft Assistant: Lucy Beaudry

TECHNICAL
Managing Editor: Leslie Schick Gorrell
Book Coordinator: Kimberly J. Smith
Senior Technical Writer: Theresa Hicks Young
Technical Writers: Sherry Solida Ford and Jean W. Lewis
Technical Assistant: Jennifer Potts Hutchings

EDITORIAL
Managing Editor: Alan Caudle
Senior Associate Editor: Stacey Robertson Marshall
Associate Editor: Kimberly L. Ross

ART
Art Director: Mark Hawkins
Senior Production Artist: Lora Puls
Lead Artist: Elaine Barry
Production Artists: Matt Davis and Dana Vaughn
Color Technician: Mark Potter
Photography Stylist: Janna Laughlin
Staff Photographer: Russell Ganser
Publishing Systems Administrator: Becky Riddle
Publishing Systems Assistants: Myra Means and Chris Wertenberger

PROMOTIONS
Associate Editor: Steven M. Cooper
Designer: Dale Rowett
Graphic Artist: Deborah Kelly

BUSINESS STAFF

Publisher: Rick Barton
Vice President, Finance: Tom Siebenmorgen
Director of Corporate Planning and Development: Laticia Mull Cornett
Vice President, Retail Marketing: Bob Humphrey
Vice President, Sales: Ray Shelgosh

Vice President, National Accounts: Pam Stebbins
Director of Sales and Services: Margaret Reinold
Vice President, Operations: Jim Dittrich
Comptroller, Operations: Rob Thieme
Retail Customer Service Manager: Wanda Price
Print Production Manager: Fred F. Pruss

Made in the United States of America.

Library of Congress Catalog Number 98-65089
International Standard Book Number 1-57486-238-3

10 9 8 7 6 5 4 3 2 1

TABLE OF CONTENTS

GARDEN INSPIRATIONS 6

GARDENER'S CARRYALL 8
Garden Caddy

SPARKLING SUN CATCHERS 10
Produce Basket Sun Catchers

BRIGHT BUTTERFLIES 11
Butterfly Light Covers

BLOOMING GIANTS 12
Hosiery Yard Flowers

RUSTIC BIRDHOUSE 14
Tin-Can Birdhouse

HERBAL DÉCOR 15
Can Herb Garden

PRETTY PLANT PEDESTAL 16
Plant Pedestal

BUBBLING BARNACLE FOUNTAIN 18
Bucket and Barnacle Fountain

IMPRESSIVE WALL ART 20
Egg Carton Sun

CHARMING RING OF VASES 22
Plastic Bottle Vases

ARTFULLY ALFRESCO TABLE 24
Concrete Patio Table

HANGING CARTON VASES 25
Hanging Carton Vases

BRILLIANT BUG 26
Big Lightbulb Bug

DECORATIVE DANGLES 28
Beaded Jar Vases and Candleholder

BLOOMING LUMINARIES 29
Can Flower Light Covers

FRIENDLY BIRD FEEDER 30
Beverage Bottle Bird Feeder

WHIMSICAL WINDFLOWERS 32
Can Windflowers

LOVABLE LAWN ORNAMENTS 34
Heart-Shaped Garden Stones

BUGGY YARD ART 35
Rusted Metal Yard Bugs

DECORATIVE TOUCHES 36

"UN-CANNY" ACCESSORIES 38
Crimped Can Frame
Can Lamp Base and Shade

MEMORABLE PHOTO TIN 40
Photo Display Tin

VIBRANT VASE 41
Stained Glass Vase

EARTHY SPHERES 42
Ornamental Balls on Crackled Stand

COUNTRY KITCHEN CANDLES 43
Votive Jars

FILE IN STYLE 44
Découpage Magazine Holder

TOTALLY TUBULAR! 46
Cardboard Tube Vases

ALL-NATURAL TOPIARY 47
Natural Topiary

PUZZLING SHADOW BOX 48
Puzzle Box Plate Frame

DANDY DOMINO FRAME 49
Domino Picture Frame

SHIMMERING FRAME 50
Gum Wrapper Frame

EARTH-FRIENDLY FRAME 52
Stick Frame with Embossed Aluminum Leaves

TABLE OF CONTENTS

DECORATIVE TOUCHES (CONTINUED) 36

DECORATIVE DESK SET 54
  Desk Set
EN VOGUE ORGANIZER 56
  Desk Organizer Set
MIRRORING NATURE 58
  Leaf-Edged Mirror and
  Stacked Spools Candlesticks
CLEARLY STYLISH CLOCK 60
  Plastic Container Clock
"FAN-TASTIC" SCONCE 61
  Fan Blade Sconce
BEAUTIFUL BEADED CANDLESTICK 62
  Bottle Bobeche and Bud Vase Candlestick
SOPHISTICATED CLOCK 64
  Container Assortment Clock
"BEARY" SPECIAL BANK 66
  Cookie Container Bank
CATNAP FLOOR MAT 67
  Vinyl Calico Cat Mat
COUNTERTOP TIER 68
  Box Lid Kitchen Organizer
SHIMMERING NAPKIN RINGS 70
  Plastic Bottle Napkin Rings

TINY TEA LIGHTS 71
  Bottle Cap Candleholders
"UN-CANNY" CHEF 72
  Can Man Chef
ARTISTIC NAPKIN HOLDER 74
  Bottle Napkin Holder
FASHIONABLY FROSTY 75
  Frosted Bottles
DANDY DRESS FORM 76
  Detergent Bottle Dress Form
RATTAN HANGING BASKET 78
  Rattan Hanging Basket
SIMPLE SACHETS 79
  Dryer Sheet Sachets
SNAZZY BEADED PINS 80
  Brooch with Curls
  Egyptian Safety Pin Brooch
  Starburst Buttons Brooch
WILD ABOUT BEADS 82
  Paper, Metal, and Wooden Beads Necklace
PETITE LAPEL VASES 83
  Perfume Bottle Lapel Pins

FUN FIX-UPS 84

DARLING DOLL CHAIR 86
  Powder Box Doll Chair
LITTLE GIRL'S KEEPSAKE BOX 88
  Girl's Keepsake Shoebox
CANINE CATCH GAME 89
  Dog Can Catch Game
MOSAIC NOTES 90
  Framed Mosaic Card Set
SASSY SALSA SERVING MAT 91
  Vinyl Serving Mat
EASY PETITE SOAPS 92
  Handmade Soaps

BLOOMING PINCUSHION 93
  Detergent Cap Pincushion
RIBBON CADDY 94
  Shoebox Ribbon Caddy
RESOURCEFUL TIEBACKS 96
  Paper Bag Chain Tiebacks
CHUNKY CANDLES 98
  Candles From Candles
NATURAL MASTERPIECE 99
  Framed Handmade Paper
SHUTTER-TOP TABLE 100
  Shutter and Mailing Tubes Table

TABLE OF CONTENTS

CREATIVE CELEBRATIONS 102

B-A-B-Y BLOCKS 104
Carton Baby Block Centerpiece

CREATIVE GIFT CARRIER 105
Gift Box With Handles

PRECIOUS HANDS MAGNETS 106
Kids' Hands Magnets

FUN PARTY PACKS 107
Frosting Container Treat Holders

PEGGY SUE PARTY PURSE 108
Tin Box Party Favor

BUBBLY BAUBLE 109
Candy Container Bubble Necklace

VALENTINE FAVORS 110
Valentine Party Favors

FAIRY-TALE PRINCE 112
Egg Carton Frog Prince

ORNAMENTAL EGG TREE 114
Decorated Egg Tree

SPRINGTIME WREATH 116
Plastic Bags Wreath

DARLING BUNNY BASKET 117
Bleach Bottle Bunny Basket

EASTER PARADE 118
Egg Carton and Lightbulb Momma Goose
and Goslings

HEARTFELT CENTERPIECE 120
Heart Centerpiece Frame

PATRIOTIC PICNIC CADDY 122
Patriotic Picnic Caddy

BRAG BAG 124
Plastic Tote Bag

"SPOOK-TACULAR" TREAT CANS 125
Cardboard Treat Cans

CREATIVE CORNUCOPIA 126
Coat Hanger Cornucopia

SNOWY VILLAGE 128
Winter Village

SHIMMERING "FOIL" TREE 130
Burnt Bag Tree

GLIMMERY GIFT TOTES 132
Découpaged Gift Bags

CRAFTY GREETINGS 133
Cards, Bookmarks, and Tags from Old Cards

HEAVENLY ANGEL PIN 134
Jewelry Angel Pin

BEJEWELED ORNAMENTS 135
Jewelry Ornaments

SWEET SNOWMAN 136
Snowman Goody Bag

PLAYFUL SNOWMEN 137
Snowman Ornaments

PATTERNS 138

GENERAL INSTRUCTIONS 156

CREDITS .160

GARDEN INSPIRATIONS

brighten your home — indoors and out — with these delightfully "recycled" garden-inspired projects. Create a handy gardening tool caddy from a plastic bucket or perky hosiery blooms for planting in a flower bed. Bring an alfresco feel to your home's interior with an "egg-ceptional" sun medallion or a tin-can herb garden to hang on the wall. With so many cheery choices, you can experience the beauty of nature anywhere!

GARDENER'S CARRYALL

*F*or the avid gardener, we've found the key to total organization! A five-gallon plastic bucket becomes an attractive outdoor carryall when covered with pieces of a pretty vinyl tablecloth. There are pockets all around, and a buttoned-on strap at the top provides loops for toting hand tools and other garden accessories.

GARDEN CADDY

Recycled items: 5-gal. plastic bucket with handle, vinyl tablecloth, twist ties, and assorted two-hole or four-hole buttons

You will also need clear silicone sealer, 2"w elastic, and a drill and bits.

Use silicone sealer for all gluing; allow to dry after each application.

1. For cover, measure bucket from below rim to bottom edge, then measure around bucket and add 2"; cut a piece of tablecloth the determined measurements. Fold one short edge of tablecloth piece 1" to wrong side and stitch in place. Beginning with short raw edge at back of bucket and trimming around handles, glue cover to bucket.

2. For pocket, measure around bucket and add 2"; cut a 12"w piece of tablecloth the determined measurement. Fold one short edge of tablecloth piece 1" to wrong side and stitch in place. Matching right sides and long edges, fold tablecloth piece in half; using a $1/2$" seam allowance, sew long edges together to form a tube. Turn tube right side out.

3. (*Note*: Apply glue liberally along bottom edge of bucket.) With seam of tube at center back and beginning with raw end, wrap and glue pocket along bottom edge of bucket.

4. Measure one side of bucket between ends of handle and add 2"; cut a piece of elastic the determined measurement. Fold each end of elastic under 1"; glue ends to bucket next to handle. Repeat for remaining side of bucket.

5. Refer to Fig. 1 to mark, then drill holes in bucket through cover and elastic.

Fig. 1

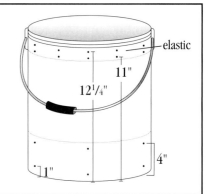

6. For each button, thread one twist-tie through holes in button; insert ends of twist tie through one hole in bucket and twist to secure.

7. To secure top sets of buttons inside bucket, twist ties together between top and bottom buttons.

8. To secure bottom sets of buttons inside bucket, twist ends of a third tie to ends of ties on buttons to connect top and bottom buttons.

SPARKLING SUN CATCHERS

*Y*our windows will sparkle and shine with these easy-to-make adornments. Great projects for creative "recycling," they're crafted from pint-size plastic berry baskets, deli plate lids, and glass paint. And with so many design possibilities, creating these colorful sun catchers is a great activity for crafters of any age!

PRODUCE BASKET SUN CATCHERS

Recycled items: pint-size plastic produce baskets and a clear plastic carry-out food container lid

You will also need utility scissors, black spray paint, craft glue, assorted colors of glass paint, $1/8$" dia. hole punch, wire cutters, and plastic-coated craft wire.

Allow paint and glue to dry after each application.

1. For each grid, use utility scissors to cut bottom from basket. Spray paint grid black.

2. Draw around grid on lid; cut out along drawn lines.

3. Apply a thin coat of glue to back of grid; glue grid to lid piece.

4. Place glued pieces, grid side up, on a flat surface. Paint desired colors inside grid.

5. Punch a hole at each top corner of sun catcher. For hanger, thread ends of a 12" length of wire, from back to front, through holes in sun catcher; curl wire ends to secure in place.

BRIGHT BUTTERFLIES

*T*hese brightly painted covers are an oh-so-easy way to turn a tiny string of lights into an exciting touch! Perfect for parties or just fun home décor, the butterfly lights start out as plain plastic beverage bottles. Slip them over the light sockets and your butterflies are ready to "flutter" their way across any spot!

BUTTERFLY LIGHT COVERS

Recycled items: 20-oz. plastic beverage bottles with caps and a string of lights

You will also need a drill and bits, black and assorted colors of spray paint, tracing paper, transparent removable tape, black permanent marker, utility scissors, white and black acrylic paint, paintbrushes, and clear acrylic spray sealer.

Refer to Painting Techniques, page 156, before beginning project. Allow paint and sealer to dry after each application.

1. For each light cover, remove cap from bottle. Drill hole through center of cap to fit over bulb socket. Spray paint bottle cap black.

2. Trace butterfly pattern pieces, page 141, onto tracing paper; cut out. Place pattern pieces around neck of bottle and tape in place; draw around outside of pattern with marker. Cut out butterfly on drawn line.

3. (*Note*: All painting is done on outside surface of bottle piece, painting in reverse order of what you see "inside" plastic.)

Paint white dots along edges of butterfly wings. Use black acrylic paint to paint antennae, eyes, lines on wings, and edges of wings over dots. Spray paint butterfly desired color, then apply two coats of sealer.

4. Replace cap on bottle top. Place light cover on lightbulb socket.

BLOOMING GIANTS

These gigantic faux yard flowers are truly works of alfresco art, cleverly made from pieces of panty hose stretched over wire coat hangers in the shapes of petals and leaves. These crafty ornaments are guaranteed to keep your garden in full bloom year-round!

HOSIERY YARD FLOWERS

Recycled items: wire coat hangers, knee-high hosiery, panty hose, and garden hose

You will also need pliers, wire cutters, assorted colors of spray paint, hose clamps, ¹/₂" dia. pipe (we used 41"- and 52"-long pipes), drill and bits, craft wire, wood-tone spray, and a utility knife.

1. For each large flower petal, use pliers to straighten hook on hanger, then form hanger into a petal shape.

2. For each small flower petal, cut hook from hanger below twisted area. Use pliers to twist wire around itself 6" to 10" from one end and shape loop to form petal and stem (Fig. 1).

Fig. 1

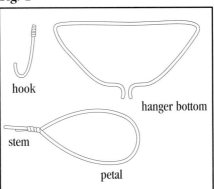

3. For each leaf, cut hook from hanger below twisted area. Twist wire around itself 1" from one end and shape loop to form leaf.

4. Cut top band from each knee-high and discard. Slide one knee-high piece onto each petal and leaf; tie to secure.

5. Paint each petal and leaf; allow to dry.

6. For each flower, place stems of petals together; tighten hose clamp around wires to secure. Insert ends of wires into one end of pipe; tie one piece of hosiery around clamp.

7. Drill one hole in each side of pipe for each leaf; place a leaf in each hole. Wrap end of hosiery around pipe, then knot around stem.

8. For each flower center, fold several knee-highs or legs from panty hose in half (fold full-length leg pieces in half three times). Wrap a length of craft wire around center of bundle and twist to secure; separate wire ends. Place bundle at center of petals, threading craft wire ends between petals; twist wire ends at back to secure. Cut through loops in bundle; separate and fluff flower center.

9. Apply wood-tone spray or paint to flower center; allow to dry.

10. Make a lengthwise cut through one side of garden hose. Cut notches in hose to fit around leaf stems. Place hose around pipe.

RUSTIC BIRDHOUSE

*O*ur crafty birdhouse is a unique home accent made using things you can gather from your kitchen or pick up at yard sales. Simply glue slats from a wooden blind around a large can and utilize an old metal pan lid to fashion the roof. A coat of paint and a few finishing touches make this project as becoming as it is earth-friendly.

TIN-CAN BIRDHOUSE

Recycled items: a large metal can (we used a shortening can), slats from a wooden blind, $1^1/2$"-long rusted bolt with nut, metal pan lid slightly larger than top of can, and a drawer pull with loop handle

You will also need a saw; household cement; red spray primer; paste floor wax; white, orange, and dark orange acrylic paint; paintbrushes; sandpaper; tack cloth; wire cutters; rusted craft wire; drill, $1^1/4$" dia. hole saw, and bits; and a hot glue gun.

Use household cement for all gluing unless otherwise indicated. Allow household cement, primer, wax, and paint to dry after each application.

1. Measure height of can. Cut pieces of slats the determined measurement. For birdhouse, glue slats around can, trimming last slat to fit if necessary.

2. Apply primer, then a thin coat of wax to house. Paint house white, sand lightly, then wipe with tack cloth.

3. Measure around can; add 6". For each wire strap, cut two lengths of wire the determined measurement. Twist wires together, then wrap around can. Twist wire ends together at back to secure; trim ends.

4. Use hole saw to drill opening through slats and can $2^1/2$" from top of can. Apply hot glue along cut edges of opening in can.

5. For perch, drill a hole to accommodate bolt $1/2$" below opening. Insert bolt through hole, then attach nut on inside of can; glue to secure.

6. Remove handle from lid. Follow *Rusting*, page 157, to paint lid. Glue drawer pull to top of lid, then lid to top of can.

HERBAL DÉCOR

*H*erb gardening need not be kept outdoors! With our unique wall "garden," you can bring the joy of growing herbs to any room in the home. Create this inventive garden container by easily attaching empty vegetable cans to an old serving tray. Accent the painted cans with rusted metal cutouts, and you're ready to plant your favorite herbs.

CAN HERB GARDEN

Recycled items: three tin cans and a metal serving tray

You will also need a drill and bits, rust-colored spray primer, acrylic paint, paintbrushes, three 1"-long plastic spacers to fit on bolts, fine-grit sandpaper, tack cloth, clear acrylic spray sealer, three ¹/₂"-long bolts with nuts, household cement, rusted metal cutouts, and desired herbs to plant.

Allow primer, paint, sealer, and household cement to dry after each application.

1. Arrange cans on tray as desired. Mark placement for bolt holes on tray and backs of cans near top edges; drill holes through tray and cans at marks.

2. Apply two coats of primer, then paint, to tray, cans, and spacers.

3. Lightly sand tray and cans for an aged finish; wipe with tack cloth. Apply two coats of sealer to tray and cans.

4. To attach each can, working from back of tray, insert bolt through tray, spacer, and hole in can; twist nut onto bolt inside can.

5. Use cement to attach cutouts to tray and cans. Plant herbs in cans.

PRETTY PLANT PEDESTAL

Here's an earth-friendly way to put a favorite plant on a pedestal! Surround a weighted stack of coffee cans with cardboard gift wrap tubes and embellish with a pretty painting technique. Wooden picture frames provide a base and top for this inventive accent piece.

PLANT PEDESTAL

Recycled items: four large, same-size coffee cans with lids; sand; small diameter cardboard gift-wrap tubes, all the same length (we used seven tubes); corrugated cardboard; and paper towel tubes

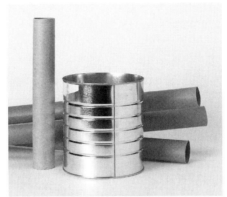

You will also need duct tape, hot glue gun, dark green and green acrylic paint, paintbrushes, clear acrylic spray sealer, wood-tone spray (optional), and two wooden frames at least 8" square with an inner wooden liner at least 1¼"w (large enough to accommodate diameter of column).

Allow paint, sealer, and wood-tone spray to dry after each application.

1. Fill one can with sand; place lids on cans. With weighted can at bottom, stack cans and tape together.

2. For column, cut gift wrap tubes in half lengthwise. Aligning one end of each tube half with bottom of can and placing tube halves close together, glue cut edges of tube halves around cans.

3. Paint column dark green, then *Dry Brush*, page 157, with green paint. Apply two coats of sealer to column.

4. If desired, apply wood-tone spray to frames.

5. For top of pedestal, cut three pieces of cardboard 1" larger on all sides than one frame; stack and glue pieces together. Cut 2"w strips, lengthwise from paper towel tubes, to cover edges of cardboard pieces; paint dark green, then *Dry Brush* with green paint. Apply two coats of sealer to tube pieces. Mitering corners to fit together and rounding tube pieces lengthwise, glue edges of tube pieces along top and bottom edges of cardboard pieces. Center and glue pedestal top to back of one frame.

6. For base, center and glue bottom of column to liner in remaining frame; center and glue pedestal top to top of column.

BUBBLING BARNACLE FOUNTAIN

*F*or a little seaside inspiration in your home, fashion our soothing barnacle fountain. The sandy-beach look of the basin comes from coating a plastic bucket with concrete, while assorted barnacles and shells create a clever disguise for the fountain pump hidden inside. Just add water and plug it in to transform the ambience of any room!

BUCKET AND BARNACLE FOUNTAIN

Recycled items: plastic bucket (we used a plastic fertilizer bucket), hardware cloth, assorted barnacles and shells, and a 3¼"h metal vegetable can

You will also need a utility knife, fountain pump kit, wire cutters, craft wire, two 10-lb. bags of quick-drying concrete mix, silicone adhesive glue, awl, hammer, and a craft knife.

1. For fountain basin, remove handle from bucket. Draw a line around bucket 6¹/₂" from bottom; cut bucket along line and discard top. Cut a notch in top edge of bucket for pump's electrical cord.

2. (*Note*: Refer to Fig. 1 for Step 2.) Measure down sides and across bottom of bucket from rim to rim and add 1"; cut a square of hardware cloth the determined measurement. Cut corners from hardware cloth.

Fig. 1

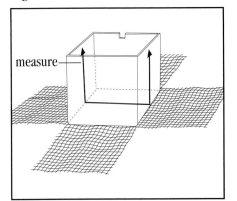

3. Referring to Fig. 2, use wire to lace corners of cloth together around bucket to within 1" from top. Bend top 1" of cloth to outside and lace in place. Form an indention in cloth at notch.

Fig. 2

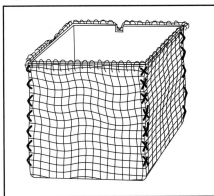

4. Mix concrete, using less water than called for in manufacturer's instructions, to form a stiff, clay-like mixture. With basin upside down, press mixture onto outside of basin working up from rim to bottom of basin (Fig. 3); allow to harden.

Fig. 3

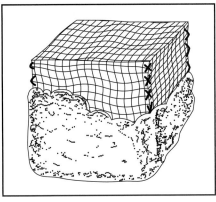

5. Glue shells to sides and rim of fountain basin, leaving notch area exposed; allow to dry.

6. (*Note*: Refer to Fig. 4 to assemble fountain platform.) Use hammer and awl to punch several holes in bottom of can, making one hole large enough to accommodate pump tubing. Cut a 4³/₄" x 10¹/₂" piece of hardware cloth and fold each short edge ¹/₂" to inside; matching folded ends, place cloth into can. Attach one end of tubing to pump; thread other end of tubing up through hole in can. With cord extending through opening in cloth, place can over pump.

Fig. 4

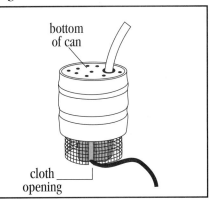

7. Use craft knife to carefully break a hole to fit tubing through bottom of one barnacle; thread tubing through hole. Position barnacle on top of can and glue in place, using glue to seal around tubing; allow to dry. Arrange and glue additional barnacles and shells to top of can; allow to dry.

8. Place fountain platform assembly in basin; place cord in notch. Glue additional shells across and below notch; allow to dry.

Get your creative juices flowing with our beautiful wall ornament! A wonderful way to enjoy the art of paper making, this fun project is crafted using paper egg carton pulp that's pressed into a metal trash can lid "mold." Use the lid's contours to inspire your creation — we fashioned a sun face because of the "ray" impressions on our lid. Terra-cotta paint and wood-tone spray give the decorative medallion its aged clay appearance.

EGG CARTON SUN

Recycled items: metal trash can lid, twelve paper egg cartons, and 10" of jute twine

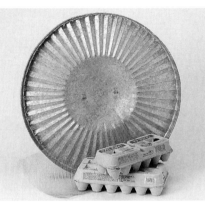

You will also need craft glue; spray primer; terra-cotta, raw sienna, and brown acrylic paint; paintbrushes; natural sponge pieces; wood-tone spray; clear acrylic spray sealer; and a hot glue gun.

Allow craft glue, primer, paint, wood-tone spray, and sealer to dry after each application.

1. Place lid upside down on level surface.

2. (*Note*: Reserve one carton cup for nose.) Use egg cartons and follow *Paper Making*, page 159, to make paper pulp. Set aside two cups of pulp for facial features.

3. Press pulp firmly into and up sides of lid to a thickness of $^1/_2$", covering inside of lid completely. Gently press pulp with a towel to remove as much moisture as possible; allow to dry. Remove dried pulp shape from lid.

4. Use remaining pulp to form crescents for eyes and mouth, and flattened circles for cheeks. For nose, cut a section from reserved egg carton cup and cover with pulp. Place eyes, mouth, cheeks, and nose on curved surface on outside of lid and allow to dry.

5. Use craft glue to adhere shapes to face.

6. Apply primer, then two coats of terra-cotta paint to both sides of sun. Follow *Sponge Painting*, page 157, to paint sun raw sienna, then brown. Apply wood-tone spray and two coats of sealer to sun.

7. For hanger, knot ends of jute; hot glue knot to back of sun.

Liven up your patio décor with our charming set of table vases! Each of five plastic juice bottles is trimmed with fabric and covered with a plastic piece cut from a two-liter soft drink bottle for outdoor durability. The vases are then attached to a flexible piece of plastic that secures around an umbrella pole with paper clips for easy placement and removal.

PLASTIC BOTTLE VASES

Recycled items: five 10-oz. white plastic beverage bottles, six clear plastic 2-liter beverage bottles, fabric scraps, paper clips, and raffia

You will also need utility scissors, spray adhesive, and household cement.

Use spray adhesive for attaching fabric; use household cement for all other gluing. Allow cement to dry after each application. Use rubber bands to hold plastic pieces in place until dry.

1. Cut tops from white bottles $1/2$" below caps and discard. Cutting from center portions of bottles, cut one $3^1/2$" x 8" piece and five 3" x 8" pieces from clear bottles. Cut five 3" x 8" pieces from fabric scraps.

2. For vases, overlapping ends at back and using spray adhesive, wrap and glue one fabric piece around each white bottle. Using household cement to secure ends at back, wrap and glue one 3" x 8" plastic piece over each fabric piece.

3. Tie lengths of raffia into a bow around each vase.

4. Place $3^1/2$" x 8" plastic piece around umbrella pole and secure with paper clips. Referring to Fig. 1 and spacing evenly, glue vases to plastic piece.

Fig. 1

ARTFULLY ALFRESCO TABLE

*F*ashioned after the expensive outdoor furniture found in specialty catalogs, our beautiful patio table provides a lot of "show" for very little dough! A plastic deli tray lid is used as a mold for the embossed concrete tabletop. After the top is attached to a wrought-iron stand, pastel paints and a cute bumblebee motif bring life to this alfresco work of art.

CONCRETE PATIO TABLE

Recycled items: a plastic deli tray lid and a wrought-iron stand

You will also need ready-mix concrete; silicone adhesive; green, yellow, white, and black acrylic paint; paintbrushes; tracing paper; transfer paper; and clear acrylic sealer.

Allow silicone, paint, and sealer to dry after each application.

1. For tabletop, follow manufacturer's instructions to mix and pour 1¹/₂" of concrete into lid; allow to harden.

2. Remove hardened tabletop from lid. Use silicone to attach tabletop to stand.

3. Paint center of table green; add yellow details. Trace bee pattern, page 141, onto tracing paper. Use transfer paper to transfer design to tabletop; paint bee. Apply two coats of sealer to tabletop.

24

HANGING CARTON VASES

*B*ring a bit of the outdoors in with these eye-catching vases! The crafty containers are created from juice cartons covered with decorative moss and preserved leaves. After rusted tin ornaments are added, these natural beauties are ready to display a bundle of your favorite flowers. What a wonderful way to lend garden appeal to any room!

HANGING CARTON VASES

Recycled items: beverage cartons with plastic pour spouts

You will also need wire cutters, rusted craft wire, nail, acrylic paint, paintbrushes, hot glue gun, greenery (we used preserved leaves, sheet moss, and reindeer moss), and rusted tin ornaments.

1. For each vase, cut a 30" length of wire; fold in half and twist to make hanger. Use nail to punch one hole in each side at top of carton. Thread hanger through holes and twist ends together; slide twisted ends to inside of carton.

2. Paint spout and allow to dry.

3. Leaving spout uncovered, glue greenery to carton, overlapping until surface is completely covered.

4. Glue or wire ornament to vase.

BRILLIANT BUG

This is one bug you won't shoo out of the garden! Our whimsical insect is attached to a stick so she can be placed in a flowerbed, garden, or anywhere for a brilliant splash of color. Wire coat hangers make realistic legs and antennae, and paper pulp smoothes the contours of the lightbulb body. Pattern-pieces cut from aluminum cans are transformed into wings, and the eyes are actually painted metal bottle caps.

BIG LIGHTBULB BUG

Recycled items: wire coat hangers, vanity-style lightbulb, long sturdy stick, two same-size plastic bottle caps, paper egg cartons, two 12-oz. aluminum beverage cans, and two metal bottle caps for eyes

You will also need wire cutters; pliers; 18-gauge craft wire; hot glue gun; utility scissors; tracing paper; spray primer; orange, pink, black, green, and white acrylic paint; paintbrushes; black permanent fine-point marker; clear acrylic spray sealer; and a utility knife.

Allow primer, paint, and sealer to dry after each application.

1. Cut one 3" length (neck) and four 12" lengths (antennae and legs) of wire from coat hangers. Use pliers to form each end of each 12" wire into a small curl; bend each wire at center to form a V.

2. Use pliers to wrap one end of 3" neck wire around center of antennae wire. Referring to Bug Assembly Diagram, page 138, place remaining end of neck wire against lightbulb socket; wrap craft wire around socket to secure neck wire in place. Place three leg wires over neck and wrap with craft wire to secure; place socket at top of stick and continue to wrap wire around stick and back up around socket. Apply glue over wrapped wires.

3. Referring to Fig. 1, use utility scissors to cut notches in plastic bottle caps. Fill each cap two-thirds full with glue; aligning notches in caps over wires, use additional glue to join caps together over antennae/neck joint to form head. Position antennae and legs as desired.

Fig. 1

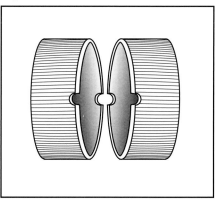

4. Use egg cartons and follow *Paper Making*, page 159, to make enough paper pulp to cover body. Press pulp onto body, sculpting areas joining body parts; allow to dry.

5. Cutting through openings in cans, cut down each can to bottom rim; cut away and discard tops and bottoms of cans. Flatten remaining can pieces. Trace wing pattern, page 141, onto tracing paper; cut out. Use pattern to cut two wings from can pieces.

6. Apply primer to wings, body, and eyes. Paint wings, legs, and antennae orange, body pink, and eyes black. Paint green and orange details on wings, body, and eyes; paint white highlights on eyes. Use marker to outline wings and add additional details. Apply two coats of sealer to wings, body, and eyes.

7. Glue eyes to each side of head.

8. Use utility knife to cut two 1" long slits in top of bug to insert wings; glue wings into slits.

DECORATIVE DANGLES

*T*ake decorating to new heights with these hanging jar vases and candleholders. All you need is wire and assorted beads to create artistic hangers designed to hold ordinary glass jars. Fill with candles or fresh or artificial flowers for interesting additions to any décor!

BEADED JAR VASES AND CANDLEHOLDER

Recycled items: clear glass jars and assorted beads

You will also need 20- and 24-gauge craft wire and wire cutters.

1. For each hanger, wrap the center of a 60" length of 20-gauge wire around top of jar twice, ending at opposite sides of jar. Thread beads onto hanger as desired. Bring wire ends together above jar and twist together 4" from ends. Repeat to add a second hanger on opposite sides of jar if desired (two-hanger vase).

2. To position beads on hanger (thin vase), wrap center of a 6" length of 24-gauge wire around hanger at each end of each bead; wrap ends around a pencil to curl.

3. To add dangles (two-hanger vase), wrap center of a length of 24-gauge wire around hanger near jar; thread beads onto wire and curl ends to secure.

4. To form hanging loop, use wire cutters to remove all but one wire at top of hanger. Thread bead onto wire, shape remaining end of wire into a loop, then push back into bead and wrap around itself to secure; wrap and curl lengths of 24-gauge wire above and below bead.

5. To add beaded crosspiece (candleholder), thread beads onto a length of 20-gauge wire; curl ends. Use lengths of 24-gauge wire to secure crosspiece to top of hanger below hanging loop.

6. Add additional wire curls and beads as desired.

BLOOMING LUMINARIES

*I*lluminate your patio party in style with this "blooming" garland of pretty lights. Simply cut aluminum cans to cover selected sockets on a string of miniature lights and curl narrow strips into "petals." These enlightening luminaries can be used for decorating anything from an umbrella to a backyard fence!

CAN FLOWER LIGHT COVERS

Recycled items: two 12-oz. aluminum beverage cans for each light cover and a string of miniature lights

You will also need utility scissors, awl, white spray primer, desired colors of spray paint, and silicone adhesive.

Allow primer, paint, and adhesive to dry after each application.

1. For each light cover, draw a line around one can 3¹/₂" from can bottom; cut top from can along line. Use awl to make a hole at center bottom of can large enough to fit over lightbulb socket.

2. Cutting through opening in can, cut down second can to bottom rim; cut away and discard top and bottom of can. Cut a 2³/₄" x 3¹/₂" rectangle from remaining piece.

3. For petals, make cuts ¹/₄" apart to within ¹/₂" from bottom of can and from one long edge of rectangle.

4. Apply primer, then two coats of paint to can pieces.

5. Wrap each petal around a pencil to curl.

6. For inner petals, overlap ends of rectangle piece ¹/₂" and glue to secure, using a paper clip to hold in place until dry. Center and glue inner petals to can bottom.

FRIENDLY BIRD FEEDER

Feeding our feathered friends has never been friendlier to Mother Nature! Instead of tossing those two-liter bottles and that empty plastic food container, use them to make this inventive birdseed dispenser that's as pretty as it is practical. Painted flower motifs lend lovely outdoor appeal to this inviting bird "restaurant."

BEVERAGE BOTTLE BIRD FEEDER

Recycled items: two clear 2-liter plastic beverage bottles with caps and a round carryout salad container bottom

You will also need household cement; drill and bits; electrical tape, desired colors of acrylic paint, including green; paintbrushes; small round dauber brush; small round spouncer; and birdseed.

Allow paint to dry after each application.

1. For seed dispenser, lightly draw a line around one bottle 9" from bottle bottom; cut top from bottle along drawn line. Refer to Fig. 1 to cut shapes from bottle top. For connector cover, cut a 1^1/$_4$" x 4 ^{1}/$_2$" piece from remaining portion of bottle; set aside.

2. Glue seed dispenser to center of salad container bottom; allow to dry.

3. For bottle connector, drill an approx. ^{1}/$_2$" dia. hole at center of each bottle cap. Tape tops of caps together. Overlapping ends, glue connector cover around taped caps and allow to dry. Twist one end of connector onto seed dispenser.

4. To paint flowers on remaining bottle, double load paintbrush with light and dark colors of paint by dipping bristles of a flat brush in water; blot on a paper towel. Dip one corner of brush into one color of paint and remaining corner of brush into second color of paint. Stroke brush back and forth on palette or foam plate until there is a gradual blending of colors at center in each brush stroke. Stroke loaded brush to make each petal on bottle, pulling brush toward you and turning project if necessary. Use spouncer to paint flower centers and dots on bottle. Paint connector cover green.

5. Fill bottle with seed; twist bottle into connector on dispenser and turn upside down to dispense seed.

Fig. 1

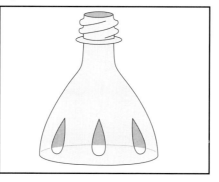

WHIMSICAL WINDFLOWERS

No one will ever guess that these brilliant spinning blooms were once aluminum cans! Pieces cut from two sizes of beverage cans form the flower centers, bent petals, and crimped leaves. The boldly painted blooms freely twirl on button-tipped nails driven into the wooden stems. What a "wind-sical" way to enliven a porch or patio!

CAN WINDFLOWERS

Recycled items: 25.4-oz. and 12-oz. aluminum beverage cans, 16"- to 18"-long $3/8$" to $1/2$" dia. sticks, buttons, and plastic tube from pump lotion bottle

You will also need utility scissors, needle-nose pliers, awl, hammer, tracing paper, craft crimper (for paper and light-weight metal), drill and $1/16$" dia. bit, floral wire, spray primer, assorted colors of spray paint, clear acrylic spray sealer, hot glue gun, and $1^{1}/4$"-long nails.

Allow glue, primer, paint, and sealer to dry after each application.

1. For each flower, draw lines around large can 1" and 5" from bottom. Cutting through opening in can, cut down side of can to 1" drawn line; cut bottom from can along line and set aside for outer petals. Cutting along 5" line, cut away and discard top of can; flatten remaining piece for leaves.

2. For outer petals of flower, make $5/8$" to $1^{1}/4$"-long cuts $1/4$" to $1/2$" apart down sides to bottom of can; twisting each petal slightly, bend petals outward and trim ends to a blunt point. Use awl to punch a hole through center of flower.

3. For each flower center, draw a line around one 12-oz. can $1/8$" to $1/4$" from bottom. Cutting through opening in can, cut down side of can to drawn line; cut bottom from can along line. For petals, make $1/8$" to $1/4$"-long cuts $1/8$" to $1/4$" apart around can; twisting each petal slightly, bend petals outward and trim ends to a blunt point. Use awl to punch a hole through center of flower center.

4. Trace leaf pattern, page 142, onto tracing paper. Use pattern to cut two leaves from flattened can piece. Follow manufacturer's instructions to crimp each leaf. Referring to pattern, use awl to punch holes in leaves.

5. For each stem, drill one hole through stick 1" from top for flower; drill two holes through stick $1/2$" apart at desired height for leaves.

6. For each leaf, thread one end of a 7" length of wire through overlapped holes in leaf; twist end around wire to secure. Thread remaining end of wire through one hole in stem, wrap around stem twice, then twist around itself to secure.

7. Apply primer to stems, leaves, flowers, flower centers, and buttons; paint pieces as desired. Apply two coats of sealer to painted pieces.

8. Cut plastic tube into $1/4$" lengths for spacers. For each flower, refer to Assembly Diagram to glue flower center to flower, then insert nail through flower and spacer, and glue nail in stem. Glue one button to head of each nail.

ASSEMBLY DIAGRAM

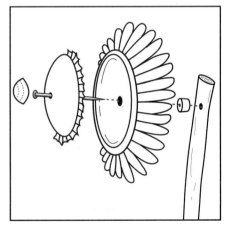

LOVABLE LAWN ORNAMENTS

*C*raft *these lovable lawn ornaments or stones from a heart-shaped candy box and some concrete mix for a sweet addition to any outdoor setting. Simply press a child's hand into the wet cement, then surround the imprint with marbles, pebbles, and acrylic jewels.*

HEART-SHAPED GARDEN STONES

Recycled items: wire clothes hangers, heart-shaped candy box, plastic shopping bags, and desired embellishments for stones (we used marbles, pebbles, and acrylic jewels)

You will also need wire cutters, ready-to-mix concrete, and sandpaper (if needed).

1. For each stone, cut pieces from hangers to fit in box.

2. With edges of bag extending over edges of box, line box with plastic bag.

3. Follow concrete manufacturer's instructions to mix and pour a thin layer of cement into lined box, pressing cement to edges. Place hanger pieces in box in a crisscross pattern; fill box with cement and allow to set briefly.

4. For child's hand print, press child's hand flat into cement. Use marbles, pebbles, and jewels to embellish heart. Allow cement to harden.

5. Remove stone from box; remove plastic bag from stone. If necessary, sand rough edges of stone.

BUGGY YARD ART

*L*end *Mother Nature a hand while you perk up your patio or garden with this earthy collection of yard ornaments. Utilize those tossed aluminum cans to make the various insect shapes, then cut lengths of metal hangers to create the stakes. Our simple rusting technique gives each bug its charming timeworn appearance.*

RUSTED METAL YARD BUGS

Recycled items: 12-oz. aluminum beverage cans and heavy-duty metal coat hangers

You will also need utility scissors, tracing paper, stylus, hammer and awl, craft wire, wire cutters, pliers, and household cement.

1. For each bug, start at opening in can and cut down one can to bottom rim; cut away and discard top and bottom of can. Flatten remaining piece. Trace desired pattern, page 142, onto tracing paper; cut out. Use pattern to cut bug from can piece.

2. Use stylus to emboss details on bug. Use hammer and awl to punch two small holes in bug head. For antennae, cut a 5" length of craft wire. From bottom, thread ends of wire through holes; use pliers to curl wire ends. Apply a small amount of cement to underside of head to secure antennae and allow to dry.

3. For stake, cut an 18" length of wire from hanger. Form a small, flat curl at one end of wire; cement bug to curl and allow to dry.

4. Follow *Rusting*, page 157, to rust bug.

DECORATIVE TOUCHES

*f*ill your home with beautiful accessories you can have fun crafting from discarded items! Light up any room with a crimped soda can lamp or an innovative sconce transformed from old ceiling fan blades. Show off lovely bath linens on a hanging rattan organizer or create a fashionable clock from a plastic food container. These projects not only look great but also help save our environment!

"UN-CANNY" ACCESSORIES

You'll never look at those empty soda cans in the same way again! Our whimsical lamp is comprised of crushed cans threaded onto a lamp kit pipe and features a matching can-trimmed lampshade. The coordinating picture frame is created using crimped pieces of aluminum cans wrapped around a flat wooden frame. These one-of-a-kind accessories are sure to spark interesting conversation in any room!

CRIMPED CAN FUN

CRIMPED CAN FRAME

Recycled items: 12-oz. aluminum beverage cans and a flat wooden picture frame

You will also need utility scissors, craft crimper (for paper and light-weight metal), hammer, and upholstery nails.

1. Cutting through openings in cans, cut down side of each can to bottom rim. Cut away and discard tops and bottoms of cans; flatten remaining pieces.

2. Measure thickness of frame edge; cut strips from can pieces the determined measurement. Rounding corners, cut remaining can pieces into desired shapes for front of frame. Follow manufacturer's instructions to crimp shapes and strips. Repeat to make enough pieces to cover frame, if necessary.

3. Using nails to secure, arrange and nail strips to edges, then shapes onto front of frame.

CAN LAMP BASE AND SHADE

Recycled items: brown paper (we used a grocery bag and brown kraft paper) and 12-oz. aluminum beverage cans for lamp base and shade

You will also need a lamp kit with base (we used a 14"h flowerpot lamp kit), découpage glue, foam brush, hammer, awl or ice pick, screwdriver, self-adhesive lampshade (we used a 7"h shade), utility scissors, craft crimper (for paper and light-weight metal), and a hot glue gun.

1. Tear pieces from brown paper. Follow *Découpage*, page 158, to cover lamp base with paper pieces; allow to dry.

2. Follow lamp kit manufacturer's instructions to assemble base and pipe of lamp.

3. Remove tabs from cans for lamp base; crush cans. Use awl to make a hole in bottom of each can through mouth in can; using screwdriver, enlarge hole to fit over lamp pipe. Leaving enough room for socket base and threading cans onto pipe, stack cans on lamp base. Complete lamp assembly.

4. Follow lampshade manufacturer's instructions to cover shade with brown paper.

5. Cutting through openings in cans for lamp shade, cut down side of each can to bottom rim. Cut away and discard tops and bottoms of cans; flatten remaining pieces.

6. Rounding corners, cut can pieces into desired shapes for edges of shade. Follow manufacturer's instructions to crimp shapes. Repeat to make enough pieces to cover shade, if necessary.

7. Arrange and glue shapes along edges of shade.

MEMORABLE PHOTO TIN

*Y*our treasured photos hold
a special place in your heart, so
shouldn't you have a special place to
store them? To create our timeworn
tin, simply spray paint an ordinary
cookie container, then attach
photocopies of news clippings with
spray adhesive. Personalize the
project with photos slipped behind
plastic covers, and finish the lid
with a pretty perfume bottle top.

PHOTO DISPLAY TIN

Recycled items: tin container with lid,
old photographs, clear plastic carry-out
food container lids, and a decorative top
for handle (we used a top from a
perfume bottle)

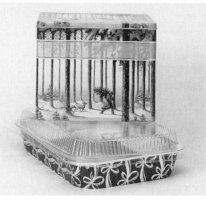

You will also need spray primer, spray
paint, spray adhesive, photocopies of news
clippings, wood-tone spray, $1/2$"w self-
adhesive magnetic strips, and a hot
glue gun.

*Allow primer, paint, and wood-tone
spray to dry after each application.*

1. Apply primer, then two coats of paint to
outside of tin and lid.

2. Use spray adhesive to adhere news
clippings to tin. Lightly spray tin and lid
with wood-tone spray.

3. For each photo cover, measure height
and width of photo and add $1/8$" to each
measurement; cut cover from plastic lid
the determined measurements.

4. For photo mounts, cut magnetic strips
into $1/2$" squares, then cut each square in
half diagonally. Remove backing and
adhere one mount to each corner of
each cover.

5. Use covers to hold photos on tin
and lid.

6. For handle, hot glue top to lid.

VIBRANT VASE

*Y*ou can achieve the intricate look of stained glass without all the work, and do something good for the environment at the same time! It's a snap to transform an ordinary glass jar into a work of art using self-adhesive leading and assorted colors of glass paint. The design is up to you, so use your imagination to create a vase that's uniquely yours.

STAINED GLASS VASE

Recycled item: large glass jar (we used a 64-oz. pickle jar)

You will also need vinegar, ⅛"w self-adhesive leading strips, and assorted colors of glass paint.

1. Use vinegar to clean outside of jar; allow to dry.

2. Removing backing from leading as you go, apply lengths of leading to form sections on jar. Apply leading around top and bottom of jar rim.

3. Using a towel to cradle jar and turning jar as sections dry, follow manufacturer's instructions to paint each section on jar.

EARTHY SPHERES

*M*other Nature provides some of the most beautiful materials for making unique crafts! To fashion our earthy spheres, simply glue pistachio shells, pebbles, sand, and seashells to balls created from crumpled, tape-wrapped paper. Display them on a crackled-finish stand made from plastic foam plates and an overturned bowl.

ORNAMENTAL BALLS ON CRACKLED STAND

Recycled items: scraps of paper, pistachio shells, pebbles, sand, seashells, two plastic foam plates, and one plastic foam bowl

You will also need painter's masking tape, hot glue gun, craft glue, brown and cream acrylic paint, paintbrushes, and crackle medium.

Allow craft glue to dry after each application. Our finished balls are 4" in diameter.

1. For each ball, crumple paper into a ball, then wrap with tape to secure.

2. For nutshell ball, hot glue pistachio shells to ball, covering it completely.

3. For pebbles ball, hot glue pebbles to ball, covering it completely.

4. For sand ball, mix two parts craft glue with one part water. Working in small sections, apply glue mixture to ball, roll ball in sand and allow to dry. Cover ball completely with sand. Hot glue seashells to ball.

5. For stand, use craft glue to attach plates together, then center and glue bottom of bowl to bottom of plates. Using brown for basecoat and cream for topcoat, follow crackle medium manufacturer's instructions to crackle stand.

6. Place balls on stand.

COUNTRY KITCHEN CANDLES

*R*eminiscent of canned goods in a country kitchen, these charming candles are the perfect way to brighten someone's day! Empty glass jars hold silk or dried items that are set permanently in a resin mixture. There's a glass candleholder inside each jar for burning votives, and raffia ties accented with orphaned earrings finish these pretty presents.

VOTIVE JARS

Recycled items: glass jars with labels removed, raffia, and earrings with posts removed

You will also need silk or dried items (we used silk asparagus spears and a dried rose hip mixture), glass candleholder smaller than jar opening, clear resin kit (if making more than one candleholder, more than one kit may be needed to complete projects), candle to fit in candleholder, and candle sealing wax.

1. For each jar, arrange desired items in bottom of jar. Position candleholder in top of jar and fill remainder of jar with items. Follow manufacturer's instructions to mix resin; using a funnel, if necessary, fill jar with resin to desired height.

2. After items in jar soak up resin and resin begins to harden, wicking (shrinking of resin) may occur; add additional resin as needed to fill jar. Allow resin to harden.

3. Place candle in candleholder.

4. Knot several strands of raffia around neck of jar. Melt sealing wax over knot; carefully press earring into hot wax, then allow wax to harden.

*O*rganize and protect your favorite magazines with this stylish publications holder made from a laundry detergent box. Simply cut the box to our specifications and découpage using scrunched tissue and decorative wallpaper scraps. It's so simple to make and adds a pretty touch to any décor!

DÉCOUPAGE MAGAZINE HOLDER

Recycled items: laundry detergent box (larger in height and width of magazine to be stored in holder), white tissue paper, and decorative wallpaper scraps (we used scraps of embossed paper)

You will also need a magazine, utility knife, white spray primer, découpage glue, foam brushes, off-white and brown acrylic paint, paintbrushes, soft cloth, and clear acrylic spray sealer.

Allow primer, glue, paint, and sealer to dry after each application.

1. For holder, draw a line around top of box 1" taller than magazine; cut top from box along drawn line. Refer to Fig. 1 to cut opening for holder.

Fig. 1

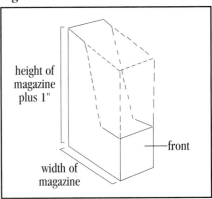

2. Apply primer to entire holder.

3. Working in small sections and covering edges, apply glue to box, then press and scrunch pieces of tissue paper into glue, covering holder completely.

4. Cut sections from wallpaper to fit on front and back of holder; glue in place. Apply an additional coat of glue to outer surface of holder.

5. Paint holder off-white; apply sealer to holder.

6. For color wash, mix two parts brown paint with one part water. Working in small sections, apply wash to holder; use cloth to wipe excess from section.

7. Apply two coats of sealer to holder.

TOTALLY TUBULAR!

*S*himmering with metallic paint accents, these unique vases were created from cardboard containers rescued from the wastebasket! We simply spruced them up with spray paint and gave each one its own distinctive flair with sponge painting and freehand motifs.

CARDBOARD TUBE VASES

Recycled items: three round cardboard containers in varying heights

You will also need ecru spray primer; round spouncers; gold, copper, and black acrylic paint; assorted paintbushes; household sponge; and clear acrylic matte sealer.

Refer to Sponge Painting, page 157, before beginning project. Allow primer, paint, and sealer to dry after each application.

1. Apply two coats of primer to containers.

2. For tallest vase, use spouncer to *Sponge Paint* a gold band of paint swirling upward around container; lightly *Sponge Paint* copper, black, then more gold paint over gold band. Swirling

upward around container, paint a gold squiggly line on each side of band.

3. For short vase, use side of household sponge to *Sponge Paint* evenly spaced, vertical gold stripes around container. Paint squiggly vertical copper lines between stripes; paint copper stars on container.

4. For remaining vase, paint gold stars on container. Lightly *Sponge Paint* container with copper paint.

5. Paint top rim of each container gold.

6. Apply two coats of sealer to containers.

ALL-NATURAL TOPIARY

*A*dd a bit of natural beauty to any spot in your home with this delightful topiary created from items you might otherwise throw away! "Planted" in a plastic yogurt container filled with plaster, this unique tree is fashioned from twigs inserted into a foam ball. Dried moss and pod or nut shell halves cover the balls, while tendrils of silk ivy give the container an alfresco touch.

NATURAL TOPIARY

Recycled items: a 24-oz. plastic container (we used a yogurt container), pieces of artificial ivy sprigs, twigs, and pod or nut shells halves

You will also need rust-colored spray primer, glossy wood-tone spray, 4" dia. plastic foam ball, utility scissors, plaster of paris, hot glue gun, and sheet moss.

Allow primer and wood-tone spray to dry after each application.

1. Apply two coats of primer to container; apply wood-tone spray to container and ivy.

2. Insert ends of twigs together into foam ball; cut twigs to desired height for topiary.

3. Follow manufacturer's instructions to mix plaster. Pour plaster into container to within 1" from top and let set briefly; insert twigs into plaster. Allow plaster to harden completely.

4. Glue moss over foam ball and over plaster in container. Glue pods to topiary; arrange and glue ivy pieces into moss in container.

47

PUZZLING SHADOW BOX

*A*ccessorizing with artistic plates is a popular decorating trend, and we've found an unusual new way to display your favorite dish. To craft our pretty "shadow box," just paint the inside of a square puzzle box and cut an opening in the lid. After covering the box with fleece-lined fabric and trimming with cord, you'll have a perfectly pleasing presentation for any plate.

PUZZLE BOX PLATE FRAME

Recycled items: a square flat box with lid (we used a 15" square puzzle box) and a plate

You will also need white spray paint, utility knife, fabric, fusible fleece, hot glue gun, decorative cord, household cement, and a heavy-duty self-adhesive picture hanger.

Use hot glue for all gluing unless otherwise indicated.

1. Spray paint inside of box bottom; allow to dry.

2. Cut an opening in center of box lid large enough to accommodate plate.

3. Refer to Fig. 1 to measure sides and top of box; cut pieces of fabric and fleece 3" larger on all sides than determined measurement. Fuse fleece to wrong side of fabric.

Fig. 1

4. Center lid on fleece side of fabric; draw around opening and remove lid. Cut out fabric 1" inside drawn line; clip corners diagonally to $1/8$" from drawn line.

5. Center lid on fleece side of fabric; glue inner fabric edges to inside of box opening. Place lid on box. Pulling fabric taut and folding at corners, glue edges to back of box.

6. Glue cord along opening and outer edges of box.

7. Use household cement to glue plate in frame; allow to dry. Attach hanger to back of frame.

DANDY DOMINO FRAME

Round up the spare dominos from the bottom of your child's toy box and use them to create this playful picture frame. The best part of our delightful project is its simplicity — just glue the tiles in a random pattern around a plain wooden frame. What a wonderfully whimsical way to brighten a room or a special friend's day!

DOMINO PICTURE FRAME

Recycled items: a flat wooden picture frame and dominos

You will also need spray primer, acrylic paint, paintbrush, and household cement.

Allow primer, paint, and household cement to dry after each application.

1. Apply primer, then two coats of paint to frame.

2. Use household cement to glue dominos to frame and allow to dry.

SHIMMERING FRAME

*U*nderneath all its shimmer and shine, our elegant photo frame has very humble beginnings! Created using materials rescued from the trash, this gorgeous home accent can be made in no time at all. A piece of cardboard covered with foil gum wrappers becomes the frame, and a textured plastic foam tray makes a lovely mat when sprayed with silver paint. Brass paper fasteners attached to each corner are an inexpensive but distinctive touch.

GUM WRAPPER FRAME

Recycled items: corrugated cardboard, plastic foam tray, lightweight cardboard (such as a cereal box), foil gum wrappers, and a 4" x 6" photograph

You will also need a craft knife and cutting mat, foam brushes, craft glue, black acrylic paint, paintbrush, silver floral spray paint, black acrylic spray paint, tape, and twelve brass paper fasteners.

Allow glue and paint to dry after each application.

1. For frame, cut an 8" x 10" piece with a 5" x 7" opening from corrugated cardboard. For mat, cut an 8" x 10" piece with a 3½" x 5½" opening from foam tray. For backing, cut an 8" x 10" piece from cereal box. For stand, cut a 2" x 10" piece from corrugated cardboard. Refer to Fig. 1 to score stand.

Fig. 1

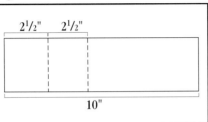
2½" 2½"
10"

2. Use foam brush to apply glue to front and edges of frame. Overlapping wrappers to cover completely, smooth crumpled wrappers onto frame. Apply black acrylic paint to frame; use a soft cloth to remove excess paint.

3. Spray paint mat silver; spray paint backing and stand black.

4. Centering in opening, tape photo to back of mat; glue frame to mat. Use a nail to punch three evenly spaced holes at each corner of frame. Matching backing to frame, punch center hole at each corner; remove backing. Leaving center holes open, and working from front to back, secure fasteners in holes. Replace backing and secure with fasteners through remaining holes.

5. Fold stand and glue to back of frame (Fig. 2).

Fig. 2

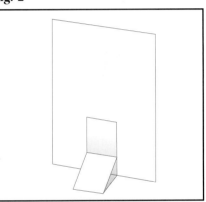

EARTH-FRIENDLY FRAME

*G*et back to nature with a beautiful home accent made with items from your backyard and recycling bin! This alfresco-inspired frame is simply constructed using four sticks held together with wire. Rust-finished aluminum-pan leaves decorate the border of the frame, and a flattened vegetable can becomes a hanging vase for a handful of dried florals.

STICK FRAME WITH EMBOSSED ALUMINUM LEAVES

Recycled items: two 10"- and two 13"-long sticks (we stripped the bark from our sticks), disposable aluminum pans, and a metal vegetable can with both ends removed

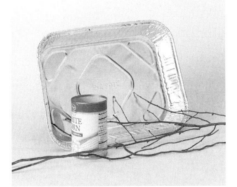

You will also need a craft saw, hot glue gun, wire cutters, 18- and 22-gauge black craft wire, tracing paper, craft foam, stylus, hammer, and a small nail.

1. Referring to Fig. 1, cut notches at each end of each stick. Using glue to secure, fit notches together to assemble frame. Crisscrossing at front, wrap lengths of 18-gauge wire around each corner of frame.

Fig. 1

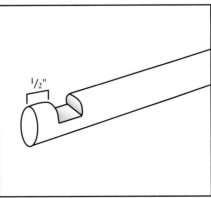

2. Trace leaf patterns, page 144, onto tracing paper; cut out. Use patterns to cut five large, six medium, and nine small leaves from aluminum pans. Place leaves on craft foam; placing patterns over leaves, use stylus to emboss veins on leaves.

3. With seam of can at center back, flatten bottom of can. Use hammer and nail to punch holes through both thickness' along bottom edge of can just above rim, and to punch a hole at each side at top of can.

4. Follow *Rusting*, page 157, to paint leaves and can.

5. "Whipstitch" 22-gauge wire through holes along bottom of can; trim ends. Cut two 9" lengths of 18-gauge wire; thread one end of each length through holes at top of can and curl ends to inside to secure. Wrap remaining ends around top of frame to hang can.

6. Cut varying lengths of 18-gauge wire. Wrap and arrange wires around frame to form vines, leaving 6" to 8" tails. Wrap wire ends around a pencil to form tendrils. Arrange and glue leaves to frame and vines.

7. For hanger, cut a 16" length of 18-gauge wire; wrap wire ends around top corners of frame.

DECORATIVE DESK SET

*G*et your home office organized with a desk set crafted from rescued refuse! Choose fabrics to complement your décor; then use them to disguise a vegetable can, a cheese box, and a piece of corrugated cardboard. Sections cut from braided leather belts become handsome trimmings for this functional "recycling" project.

DESK SET

Recycled items: a vegetable can, cereal box, braided leather belts, bottom of a 2-lb. cardboard cheese box, and corrugated cardboard

You will also need acrylic spray primer, acrylic paint to coordinate with fabric, paintbrush, two coordinating fabrics (one for letter holder liner), spray adhesive, hot glue gun, burlap, and felt to coordinate with fabrics.

Allow primer and paint to dry after each application. Use hot glue for all gluing unless otherwise indicated.

PENCIL CUP

1. Apply primer, then paint to inside of can.

2. Measure height and circumference of can; cut a piece of cardboard from cereal box the determined measurements. Draw around cardboard piece on wrong side of fabric; cut out $1/2$" outside drawn lines.

3. Apply spray adhesive to wrong side of fabric. Center cardboard piece on fabric; folding corners, smooth fabric edges to back of cardboard. Glue covered cardboard around can.

4. Measure around can; cut a piece from one belt the determined measurement. Matching ends at back, glue belt piece around can.

LETTER HOLDER

1. Carefully unfold cheese box. Cut a piece of fabric for liner, 1" larger on all sides than unfolded box. Place fabric right side down on a flat surface. Apply spray adhesive to inside of box. Center unfolded box, adhesive side down, on fabric; press firmly to secure.

2. Trim fabric $1/2$" outside edges of box; glue edges to outside of box.

3. Repeat Step 1 to cover outside of box with coordinating fabric; trim fabric even with edges of box. Refold box and glue to secure.

4. Fasten one belt around top of box; trim end and glue in place.

DESK PAD

1. Cut an 18" x 24" piece of corrugated cardboard, a 20" x 26" piece of fabric, and a $17^1/_2$" x $23^1/_2$" piece of felt.

2. For pad, apply spray adhesive to wrong side of fabric. Center cardboard piece on fabric; folding corners, smooth edges to wrong side of cardboard.

3. Glue lengths of belts along edges of pad. For note holder, glue buckle end of one belt at top left corner of pad.

4. Cut four 6" squares of burlap. Press each square in half diagonally. Arrange triangles across corners of pad; fold edges to back of pad and glue to secure.

5. Apply spray adhesive to one side of felt. Center and smooth felt over back of pad.

EN VOGUE ORGANIZER

*O*ur nifty desk organizer shelf boasts a lot of animal magnetism! Juice cans and a cardboard fabric bolt are covered with trendy animal print wallpaper to fashion the "cubbies" and shelf, and a tuna can becomes a catchall container. Coordinating covered albums keep important phone numbers, addresses, and lists at your fingertips. This in-style, fun-to-create project makes getting organized a breeze!

DESK ORGANIZER SET

Recycled items: five 46-oz. juice cans, 6-oz. tuna can, large scraps of coordinating wallpaper, fabric bolt, assorted buttons, small album or address book, and a brown paper bag

You will also need painter's masking tape, brown spray paint, craft glue, hot glue gun, decorative-edge craft scissors, and a black marker.

Use craft glue for all gluing unless otherwise indicated; allow to dry after each application.

1. Adhere tape to cans below rims. Spray paint rims and insides of cans brown and allow to dry; remove tape.

2. For each can, measure height of can between rims; measure circumference of can and add $^1/_2$". Cut a piece of wallpaper the determined measurement; overlapping ends, glue around can (top).

3. For shelf, use wallpaper to wrap bolt gift-wrap style (with overlap at bottom) using glue to secure.

4. Hot glue large cans together and to bottom of shelf. Hot glue buttons to can rims at front of organizer.

5. For each decorative cover, measure length and width of outside cover of album or address book and add 1" to length; cut a piece of wallpaper the determined measurements. Center and glue wallpaper piece to album cover, folding and gluing ends to inside of cover.

6. For album label, use craft scissors to cut a rectangle from paper bag; use marker to write on label. Glue label to front of cover.

MIRRORING NATURE

*M*irrors and candles add life to any room, especially when they're garden-inspired. Create these ornate accents by cutting leaf shapes from flattened aluminum cans. Apply a painted faux-patina finish, then attach the leaves around a framed mirror and onto candlesticks to complete this alfresco project.

LEAF-EDGED MIRROR AND STACKED SPOOLS CANDLESTICKS

LEAF-EDGED MIRROR

Recycled items: aluminum beverage cans, newspaper, and mirror with a wooden frame

You will also need utility scissors; tracing paper; decorative-edge craft scissors (we used pinking shears); craft foam; stylus; $1/8$" dia. and $1/4$" dia. hole punches; rust-colored spray primer; copper, bronze, green, and pearl mint green acrylic paint; paintbrushes; natural sponge pieces; painter's masking tape; clear acrylic spray sealer; small brass nails; small $3/8$" dia. brass washers; and a hammer.

Refer to Painting Techniques, page 156, before beginning project. Allow glue, primer, paint, and sealer to dry after each application.

1. Cut through openings in beverage cans and down to bottom rims; cut away and discard tops and bottoms of cans. Flatten can pieces.

2. Trace leaf pattern, page 143, onto tracing paper; cut out. Using pattern and craft scissors, cut leaves from can pieces to fit around frame.

3. To emboss each leaf, place leaf on craft foam. Place pattern on leaf, then, pressing firmly to make indentions, use stylus to draw over embossing lines on pattern and to make mark for hole in leaf. Punch a $1/8$" hole in each leaf where indicated. Apply primer to front and back of leaf.

4. Paint leaf copper, then *Sponge Paint* with bronze paint. For faux-patina, mix unequal parts of green and mint green paint; lightly *Sponge Paint* mixture onto leaves.

5. Use tape and newspaper to mask mirror for painting; repeat Step 4 to paint frame.

6. Apply two coats of sealer to leaves and frame; remove paper and tape.

7. For spacers, use $1/4$" dia. hole punch to cut one circle from craft foam for each leaf.

8. Arrange leaves, embossed sides up, along edges of frame. To attach each leaf, insert nail through center of one spacer, through one washer, then into hole in leaf; hammer nail into frame.

STACKED SPOOLS CANDLESTICKS

Recycled items: heavy cardboard (such as the back of a writing tablet) and aluminum beverage cans

For each candlestick, you will also need utility scissors; pinking shears; craft glue; large wooden spools (ours measure $1^1/2$" dia. x 2"h); two $3/4$"-long pieces of $3/8$" dia. dowel; drill and $1/32$" bit; 2" dia. wooden candle cup; 1"-long thin brass screws; tracing paper; decorative-edge craft scissors (we used pinking shears); craft foam; stylus; $1/8$" dia. and $1/4$" dia.

hole punches; rust-colored spray primer; copper, bronze, green, and pearl mint green acrylic paint; paintbrushes; natural sponge pieces; $3/8$" dia. brass washers; and clear acrylic spray sealer.

Refer to Candlestick Assembly Diagram, page 138, to assemble candlesticks. Allow glue, primer, paint, and sealer to dry after each application.

1. For base, use utility scissors to cut two $3^1/2$" dia., one $3^1/4$" dia., and one 3" dia. circle from cardboard; use pinking shears to cut one $2^1/2$" dia. circle. Glue $3^1/2$" dia. circles together, then center and glue $3^1/4$" dia., 3" dia., then $2^1/2$" dia. circles on top.

2. Glue spools together for spindle. Glue dowel pieces into holes at top and bottom of spindle. Drill a hole through center of dowel pieces, base, and candle cup. Insert one screw through bottom of base and into hole in dowel at bottom end of spindle.

3. Follow Steps 1 – 3 of Leaf-Edged Mirror to make five leaves.

4. Apply primer to front and back of leaves, candlestick, and candle cup. Follow Step 4 of Leaf-Edged Mirror to paint leaves, candlestick, and candle cup.

5. For spacer, use $1/4$" dia. hole punch to cut a circle from craft foam.

6. Insert screw through candle cup, center of spacer, holes in leaves (embossed sides up), and washer, then into hole in dowel at top of candlestick; arrange leaves, then tighten screw. Apply two coats of sealer to candlestick.

CLEARLY STYLISH CLOCK

*D*on't throw away your take-out food container — use the clear lid as the face on an attractive timekeeper! Choose a pretty picture (ours came from an old calendar), for the background, attach a clock kit, and voilà — you'll be telling time in style!

PLASTIC CONTAINER CLOCK

Recycled items: a calendar page (at least the same width and height as the diameter of carry-out container lid), cardboard, and a round clear plastic carry-out food container lid with a raised center (we used a 10" dia. x 1¼" deep lid)

You will also need spray adhesive, drawing compass, clock kit, and household cement.

1. Apply spray adhesive to wrong side of calendar page; adhere to cardboard. For background, trace around lid on calendar page; cut out.

2. For clock face, use compass to mark a smaller circle at center of background to fit raised center of lid; carefully cut out and set outer ring aside. Use spray

adhesive to adhere right side of clock face to inside of lid.

3. Cut a hole through center of clock face and lid to accommodate clock kit.

4. Follow manufacturer's instructions to assemble clock kit on clock face.

5. Aligning image, use household cement to glue outer ring to back of lid along edges; allow to dry.

"FAN-TASTIC" SCONCE

*N*ot sure what to do with that ceiling fan with the broken motor? Don't trash the blades— transform them into our eye-catching candle sconce! A wooden bracket and a fan blade piece create a "shelf" for a candlestick and a hurricane globe. An aged paint finish gives this novel fixture its elegance.

FAN BLADE SCONCE

Recycled items: two wooden ceiling fan blades (with hardware removed), wooden candlestick, and a hurricane globe

You will also need a saw, wood glue, 5" x 7" decorative wooden shelf bracket, drill, ³/₄"-long wood screws, wood filler, sandpaper, tack cloth, brush-on primer, paintbrushes, green and white acrylic paint, and a heavy-duty picture hanger.

Allow wood glue, wood filler, primer, and paint to dry after each application.

1. For shelf, cut a 5¹/₂"-long piece from narrow end of one fan blade. Matching back edges, center and glue shelf on 5" edge of bracket, then candlestick on shelf.

2. Working from back, drill pilot holes, then use screws to attach shelf to remaining blade for sconce.

3. Fill holes with wood filler. Sand sconce, then wipe with tack cloth.

4. Apply primer, then green paint to sconce. Lightly *Dry Brush*, page 157, sconce with white paint.

5. Attach hanger to back of sconce.

6. Place globe over candlestick.

BEAUTIFUL BEADED CANDLESTICK

BOTTLE BOBECHE AND BUD VASE CANDLESTICK

Transform a simple bud vase into an elegant tabletop candlestick in less time than it takes to set the table! Using our flower pattern as a guide, trace and cut out the bobeche design from the top of a two-liter plastic beverage bottle, then glue it to the top of a glass bud vase. For a sparkling finishing touch, trim the rim of the bottle section with beads and attach beaded dangles to the petals.

Recycled items: clear plastic 2-liter beverage bottle, bud vase, and clear beads (we used a beaded Christmas garland)

You will also need tracing paper, fine-point permanent marker, household cement, beading needle, and clear nylon thread.

Allow household cement to dry after each application.

1. For bobeche, trace petals pattern, page 143, onto tracing paper; cut out. Place pattern over neck of bottle. Use marker to draw around pattern; cut out petals inside drawn lines.

2. Bend every other petal up to rim and glue in place. Use a large needle to pierce a small hole near tip of each remaining petal.

3. Using beading needle and thread, string a length of beads to fit around rim of bottle section, covering ends of glued petals; knot and trim ends. With bottle rim turned upside down to fit into vase, glue bobeche in vase; allow to dry.

4. For each dangle, string a length of beads onto thread, running one end of thread around last bead and back up through remaining beads. Insert ends of thread through hole in tip of petal to attach each dangle; knot and trim ends.

SOPHISTICATED CLOCK

An elegant clock need not cost you a fortune — just gather a few kitchen discards and make one yourself! Assorted cardboard containers and plastic bottles are used to construct the clock. Decorative wood pieces and dry brush painting give the timepiece its sophisticated finish and detail.

CONTAINER ASSORTMENT CLOCK

Recycled items: one half-gallon size paper beverage carton, adult-size shoebox lid, four 20-oz. plastic beverage bottles, two round wooden beads, two plastic game pieces (we used pawns from a chess game), and a box for body (we used an ice cream waffle bowl box)

You will also need utility scissors, hot glue gun, decorative wooden cutout, craft knife, Create-A-Clock® clock kit, paintable latex caulk, spray primer, cream and brown acrylic paint, paintbrushes, and clear acrylic spray sealer.

Allow primer, caulk, and paint to dry after each application.

1. For topper, draw around carton 4¼" below top of carton; cut along drawn lines. Glue top of carton closed. Cut a triangle "gable" from bottom carton piece to fit over indented "triangle" on front of topper; glue in place. Glue wooden cutout to gable.

2. For "shelves," cut shoebox lid in half width-wise. For legs, draw around each beverage bottle 4½" below top; cut along drawn lines and discard bottoms. For decorative spindles, glue one bead to top of each game piece.

3. Cut a hole in front of clock to snugly accommodate clock kit.

4. With lip of shelf to front, glue cut edges of legs to bottom side of bottom shelf. Centering pieces, glue body to top of bottom shelf, bottom of top shelf to top of body, and topper to top of top shelf. Glue spindles to front corners on top shelf.

5. Apply caulk along all joints and crevices. Apply two coats of primer, then cream paint, to clock. *Dry Brush*, page 157, clock with brown paint, then apply two coats of sealer.

6. Insert clock kit in clock.

"BEARY" SPECIAL BANK

*S*aving money is lots of fun for little ones with our "beary" special bank! A plastic cookie container is cleverly découpaged with torn pieces of brown paper bags, then painted. The bear's face comes alive with rosy cheeks and twinkling eyes, and his card stock "tummy" displays a precious caption accented with honeybee buttons.

COOKIE CONTAINER BANK

Recycled items: plastic bear-shaped cookie container with lid and lightweight brown paper bags

You will also need a black permanent marker; drill and small bits; utility knife; découpage glue; dark brown, black, pink, and white acrylic paint; paintbrushes; decorative-edge craft scissors; tan card stock; hot glue gun; three bee shank buttons with shanks removed; and clear acrylic spray sealer.

Allow paint and sealer to dry after each application. Use découpage glue for all gluing unless otherwise indicated.

1. With lid securely in place on container, use marker to draw a $1/8$" x $1 1/2$" rectangle at center of lid for coin slot. Remove lid from container and place on a piece of wood; drill holes across the whole line to make slot. Use utility knife to smooth sides of slot.

2. Tear brown bags into small pieces; follow découpage glue manufacturer's instructions to adhere pieces to container (do not cover threads for lid).

3. Leaving muzzle unpainted, paint container dark brown. Following contours of container, paint black eyes, nose, claws, and mouth, and pink cheeks; paint a white highlight in each eye.

4. For sign, use craft scissors to cut out a shape from card stock to fit on front of container; use marker to write message on sign. Glue sign to container.

5. Apply two coats of sealer to bank; replace lid on bank. Hot glue buttons to sign.

CATNAP FLOOR MAT

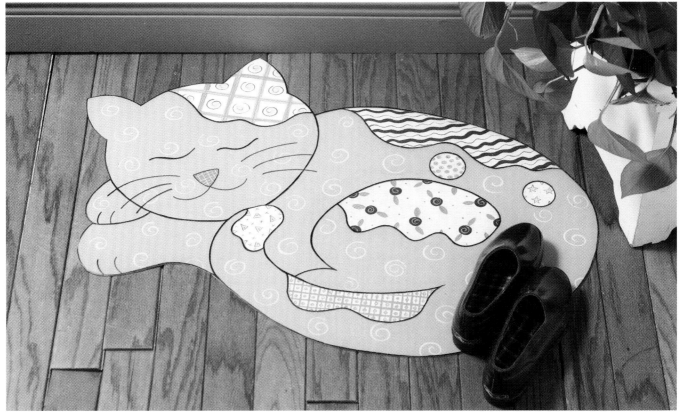

*T*his happy kitty just loves to lie around! Made from a piece of vinyl flooring, our inventive project is both inexpensive and earth-friendly. The easily transferred design is outlined with black marker and painted, then detailed with paint-pen swirls. The resulting patchwork look makes our calico cat feel at home in any room.

VINYL CALICO CAT MAT

Recycled item: a 2' x 3' piece of vinyl floor covering

You will also need white primer; dark yellow colored pencil; black permanent marker; utility scissors; dark yellow,

white, and desired colors of acrylic paint; assorted paintbrushes; light yellow fine-point paint pen; and clear acrylic spray sealer.

Work on wrong side of vinyl to make mat. Allow primer, paint, and sealer to dry after each application.

1. Apply two coats of primer to vinyl piece.

2. Use a yardstick and yellow pencil to draw a grid with 2" squares on vinyl. Using cat pattern, page 144, use pencil to draw pattern, square by square, on vinyl; use marker to draw over pattern lines. Use utility scissors to cut out mat.

3. Paint main area of cat yellow; paint patches white. For color wash, mix one part yellow paint with one part water; apply wash to patches. Paint details on patches. Use paint pen to draw swirls on mat.

4. Use marker to draw over pattern lines again.

5. Apply three or more coats of sealer to mat.

COUNTERTOP TIER

Kiss that kitchen clutter goodbye with our handy countertop organizer! It's so easy to fashion shelves from corrugated cardboard and shoebox lids. Strips of painted cardboard create the dimensional look along the edges. Plain glass jars filled with layers of dried vegetables and rice provide a "stand" to support the shelves, which are ideal for organizing spices, coupons, or other lightweight kitchen items.

BOX LID KITCHEN ORGANIZER

Recycled items: corrugated cardboard, three box lids in graduated sizes (we used shoebox lids), two jars with lids, and brown paper bags

You will also need a utility knife; craft glue; assorted colors of acrylic paint to coordinate with your kitchen (we used yellow, cream, and green); paintbrushes; and assorted beans, peas, corn, and rice.

Allow paint and glue to dry after each application.

1. For each tray, cut a piece of cardboard ³/₈" larger on all sides than one box lid; center and glue lid upside down on cardboard. Paint trays and jar lids yellow.

2. For each tray, cut three strips of cardboard in graduated widths to fit each side of tray.

3. For each corner piece, refer to Fig. 1 to cut pieces from cardboard to fit corners and to bend shape along center.

Fig. 1

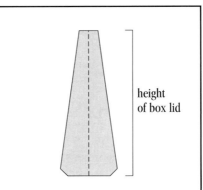

height of box lid

4. Cut down seams of bags; cut away and discard bottoms. Crumple, then smooth remaining paper bag pieces. To line each tray, refer to Fig. 2 to measure inside of tray (A and B). Cut a piece of paper bag the determined measurement; from each corner, cut a square the depth of the tray (C). Glue paper liner in lid.

Fig. 2

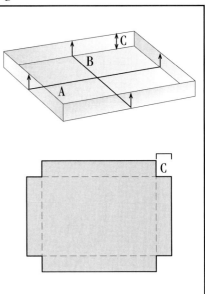

5. *Dry Brush*, page 157, liners and narrow cardboard strips yellow, wide strips cream, and center strips and corner pieces green.

6. Stack and glue strips, then corners to sides of lids, to complete trays.

7. For support column, fill jars completely with layers of beans, peas, corn, and rice; replace lids on jars.

8. With back edges of trays aligned and beginning with largest tray, stack and glue trays together to complete organizer.

SHIMMERING NAPKIN RINGS

*C*reate artistic napkin rings with sections cut from a plastic hairspray bottle. Simply glue shoestring pieces around the top and bottom edges of each ring and cover with crumpled paper. After adding some black paint, rub-on metallic finish, and assorted beads, these eye-catching accents will be appreciated by all ... including Mother Nature!

PLASTIC BOTTLE NAPKIN RINGS

Recycled items: plastic hair spray bottle, round shoestrings, tissue paper, aluminum window screen scrap, and assorted beads

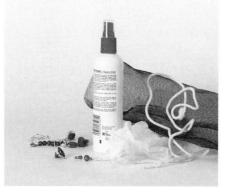

You will also need craft glue, paintbrush, black acrylic paint, metallic gold rub-on wax finish, and wire cutters.

1. For each napkin ring, cut a 1" ring from hair spray bottle.

2. Measure around ring; cut two pieces from shoestrings the determined measurement. Glue shoestring pieces around top and bottom edges of ring and allow to dry.

3. Cut a piece of tissue paper large enough to cover entire ring; crumple tissue paper, then smooth flat. Use paintbrush to apply a thin layer of glue to entire ring; overlapping edges to inside, cover ring with paper and allow to dry.

4. Paint ring black and allow to dry, then follow manufacturer's instructions to apply rub-on finish to ring.

5. Pull two lengths of wire from screen. Center and wrap wire lengths around ring; twist to secure. Thread one bead onto end of each wire. Wrap each wire end around a needle several times to secure bead in place; trim ends.

TINY TEA LIGHTS

*H*ere's a great gift idea for Mother's Day or a birthday! These candleholders can be crafted in minutes by spray painting the top portion and cap of a plastic juice bottle. Glued-on preserved leaves, bits of moss, flowers, and berries enhance the decorative base, topped with a glass votive holder. What an illuminating way to bring a little cheer to someone's day!

BOTTLE CAP CANDLEHOLDERS

Recycled items: plastic juice bottles with caps

You will also need utility scissors; green spray paint; hot glue gun; preserved leaves, moss, berries, and small flowers; and glass votive holders with candles.

1. For each cap candleholder, cut top from bottle $1/2$" below cap.

2. Paint candleholder green; allow to dry.

3. Glue leaves, then moss, berries, and flowers along inside of candleholder, bending leaves outward.

4. Place glass votive holder in cap candleholder.

"UN-CANNY" CHEF

We've cooked up a recipe for fun in the kitchen with our fanciful can man chef! Simply follow the directions to crush an aluminum can, then create his arms and legs using craft foam. Holding his "soup pot" filled with miniature artificial vegetables, this humorous culinary helper is sure to stir a laugh or two!

CAN MAN CHEF

Recycled items: white craft foam scraps, 12-oz. aluminum beverage can, 6" x 10" white fabric strip, and a cardboard egg carton

You will also need tracing paper; white spray primer; hot glue gun; white, red, flesh, brown, black, and blue acrylic paint; paintbrushes; black fine-point permanent marker; satin and glossy clear acrylic spray sealer; 8" of clear nylon thread; utility scissors; white bumpy chenille stem; miniature artificial vegetables; natural sponge piece; and a miniature fork and spoon.

Refer to Painting Techniques, page 156, before beginning project. Allow primer, paint, and sealer to dry after each application.

1. Trace patterns, page 143, onto tracing paper; cut out. Using patterns, cut two hands and two shoes from foam. Cut four $1/2$" x 2" pieces of foam for arms and legs and one $1^1/2$" x $4^1/4$" piece for hatband.

2. Remove tab from can; set aside. Referring to Fig. 1, bend top of can down, bend bottom of can in opposite direction, then fold top points to back.

Fig. 1

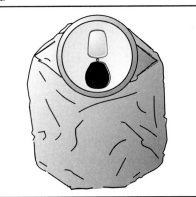

3. Spray can with primer. For body, glue arms and legs to can, then paint body white. Paint visible area inside "mouth" red; paint face and hands flesh. Use finger to lightly paint red cheeks and nose on face. Using oval hole in can tab as a template, draw eyes on face. Paint eyes white; paint iris' brown with white highlights.

4. Use black marker to draw eyelashes and eyebrows on face, coat flap and "stitches" down front of body, details on shoes, and lines on hatband. Paint black *Dots* on coat flap for buttons. Spray body with two coats of satin sealer.

5. Glue hands to ends of arms and shoes to ends of legs. For hanger, knot ends of clear thread together; glue knot to top of head.

6. Matching long edges, fold fabric strip in half. Gathering to fit, glue raw edges of strip along one long edge on wrong side of hatband. Glue ends of hatband together to form a circle; overlap fabric edges and glue to secure. Thread hanger through hat; glue hat on head.

7. For mustache, cut one bump from chenille stem; bend in half. Trim chenille at bend and curl up ends. Glue mustache to face.

8. For vegetable pot, cut one cup from egg carton; spray cup with primer. Lightly *Sponge Paint* pot blue; spray with two coats of glossy sealer. Arrange and glue vegetables in pot. Glue pot to chef, then glue arm around pot; glue fork and spoon in opposite hand.

ARTISTIC NAPKIN HOLDER

Transform an ordinary plastic salad dressing bottle into our lovely napkin holder. Just cut the desired shape from the bottle and glue silk flower petals to the inside. A layer of crumpled wax paper applied with glue gives everything an elegant crackled appearance.

BOTTLE NAPKIN HOLDER

Recycled items: a plastic salad dressing bottle, silk flowers, and silk leaves on stems

You will also need a black permanent fine-point marker, dimensional paint, spray adhesive, waxed paper, craft glue, and a foam brush.

1. Use marker to draw desired shape for napkin holder on bottle; cut out shape just inside drawn lines.

2. Remove flowers from stems. Separate petal layers into single flowers and press flat. Use paint to cover hole at center of each flower and allow to dry.

3. Apply adhesive to right side of flowers, stems, and leaves, and adhere to inside of holder.

4. Crumple waxed paper, then smooth flat. Mix one part glue with one part water; use foam brush to apply mixture to inside of holder. Press waxed paper onto inside of holder and allow to dry. Trim paper edges even with holder.

FASHIONABLY FROSTY

*D*on't toss those condiment bottles and honey jars — transform them into beautiful home accents! Simply arrange a variety of stickers on each bottle and spray on a frosted glass finish. When the stickers are removed, clear motifs remain, creating one-of-a-kind containers with endless decorative possibilities.

FROSTED BOTTLES

Recycled items: clear glass bottles

You will also need self-adhesive stickers in desired shapes, frosted glass spray finish, and a craft knife.

1. Clean bottles with soap and water and allow to dry.

2. Adhere stickers to bottles as desired.

3. Follow manufacturer's instructions to apply frosted finish to bottles.

4. Use craft knife to carefully remove stickers from bottles.

Reminiscent of days gone by, this dainty dress form will bring old-fashioned charm to any room. We started with a plastic detergent bottle covered with fabric and slid it onto a stand made from a spool-covered dowel and a wooden plaque. Glued-on bits of colorful trim and lace create the bustle and floweret.

DETERGENT BOTTLE DRESS FORM

Recycled items: 19-oz. liquid dish detergent bottle (with cap and all labels removed), small wooden spools, and decorative lace and trims

You will also need a nail; cotton batting; fabric (we used a tightly-woven muslin); craft glue; foam brush; wooden plaque (we used a 5¼" x 7¼" oval plaque); brown, ivory, and pink acrylic paint; paintbrushes; and 11¾" of ¼" dia. dowel.

Refer to Painting Techniques, page 156, before beginning project. Working in small sections, use foam brush to apply a thin layer of glue to surface of bottle before covering with fabric. Allow glue and paint to dry after each application.

1. Use nail to punch a ¼" dia. hole in center bottom of bottle.

2. Cut a circle of batting ¼" larger than bottle opening; cut a 2" circle of fabric. Center and glue batting circle on wrong side of fabric circle. Place circles, batting side down, over bottle opening. Cutting notches and trimming fabric as necessary, smooth fabric over glue.

3. To cover top of bottle (bodice), cut two 4" x 5½" pieces of fabric. Working from center outward, smooth one fabric piece onto bottle back, notching and overlapping edges of fabric as needed; repeat to glue remaining fabric piece to bottle front.

4. To cover lower section of bottle (skirt), cut a 6½" x 10" piece of fabric. Beginning at front and working from center outward, smooth fabric piece onto bottle, overlapping edges of fabric at center back. Cutting notches and overlapping fabric, smooth fabric onto bottom of bottle.

5. For stand, stack and glue spools to center of plaque. Using brown paint for basecoat and ivory for topcoat, follow *Aged Finishes* to paint stand. Follow *Dry Brush* to paint stand with pink.

6. Insert one end of dowel into spools; glue in place. Apply glue to opposite end of dowel; place bottle over dowel, so that end of dowel adheres to batting inside bottle neck.

7. Overlapping, folding, and trimming as necessary, glue lengths of lace and trim to bottle, covering raw edges of fabric and forming decorative accents such as collar, bustle, and floweret, to complete dress form.

RATTAN HANGING BASKET

If you're running out of storage space in the bathroom, this crafty project is for you! Our triple-tiered hanging basket features "shelves" made from rattan plate holders connected by beaded wire. Tiny dangles add decorative appeal to this pretty and practical bathroom accessory.

RATTAN HANGING BASKET

Recycled items: three rattan paper plate holders, paper bag, and assorted beads

You will also need spray primer, spray paint, wire cutters, craft wire, two pony beads, and a 20mm berry bead.

1. Apply primer, then paint to each holder, allowing to dry after each application.

2. Place one holder upside down on bag; draw around holder, then cut out circle ¹/₄" outside line. Fold circle in half twice to divide into quarters; unfold. For wire placement, place each holder upside down on circle; mark rim of holder at each crease in paper.

3. For hanger wires, cut four 30" lengths of wire. Thread three assorted beads onto one end of one wire 2" from end of wire.

Bring end of wire around bottom bead, thread wire back through two remaining beads, and twist wire end around itself to secure. Thread opposite end of wire through rim of bottom holder at one mark. Thread 6" of beads onto wire; thread wire through rim of middle holder at mark. Thread 6" of beads onto wire; thread wire through rim of top holder at mark. Thread 9" of beads onto wire; bend wire to hold in place. Repeat to add remaining three hanger wires.

4. For hanger, thread wire ends together above top holder, through one pony bead, berry bead, and remaining pony bead. Form a loop and twist wire ends around wires to secure.

5. For each dangle, thread three beads onto one end of a 3" length of wire; bring end of wire around bottom bead, thread back through two remaining beads, and twist wire end around itself to secure. Thread remaining end of wire through rim of holder and through one bead; twist wire around itself under bead to secure and trim wire end.

SIMPLE SACHETS

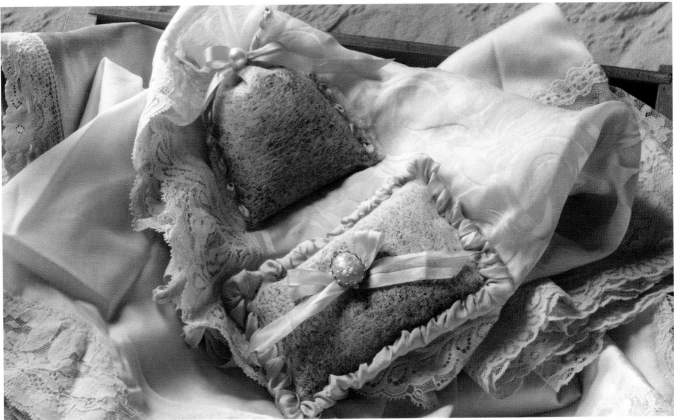

*D*on't toss those used dryer sheets into the trash ... give them a new job as dainty sachets filled with lavender! Simply glue the edges of dryer sheet pieces together and secure with decorative ribbon stitching. Fill the pouch with dried lavender. Adorn with bows and assorted jewelry.

DRYER SHEET SACHETS

Recycled items: dryer sheets and pieces of jewelry

You will also need craft glue, narrow and wide silk ribbon (we used 7mm and 13mm wide ribbons), and dried lavender.

Allow glue to dry after each application.

1. For each sachet, use a very cool iron to press dryer sheet.

2. For bag sachet, matching ends, fold a 3¹/₄" x 9" piece of dryer sheet in half; glue long edges together.

3. Using narrow ribbon and knotting ribbon at top and bottom corners, work *Running Stitches*, page 158, along sides of bag. Fill bag with lavender; gather top over lavender. Tie a length of narrow ribbon into a bow around gathers; glue a piece of jewelry to knot of bow.

4. For pillow sachet, cut two 3¹/₄" x 4¹/₂" pieces of dryer sheets and place together; glue short edges and bottom of pieces together. Fill sachet with lavender, then glue top edges together.

5. Using wide ribbon, work *Whipstitches*, page 158, along edges of sachet; knot and trim ends. Tie a length of wide ribbon into a bow; glue to front of sachet. Glue a piece of jewelry to knot of bow.

SNAZZY BEADED PINS

*T*ransform miscellaneous beads and buttons into fashionable jewelry. Thread loose beads onto small safety pins and combine them with buttons and pearls to create the snazzy designs. Pinned to your jacket or sweater, they're wonderful accessories for any occasion.

SAFETY PIN JEWELRY

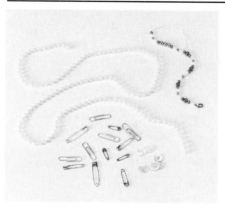

BROOCH WITH CURLS

Recycled items: two jumbo paper clips; 1¹/₂"-long safety pin; 4mm gold beads; one large, two medium, and two small two-hole buttons; and one large and one small shank button

You will also need 24-gauge gold jewelry wire, wire cutters, two pairs of needle-nose pliers, and clear silicone adhesive.

Using two pairs of pliers makes it easier to work with small paper clip and wire pieces. Use silicone for all gluing; allow to dry after each application.

1. Use pliers to straighten paper clips; cut two 1" lengths for short dangles, two 3½" lengths for curled dangles, and one 2½" length for straight dangle. Form a small loop, large enough to thread onto safety pin, at one end of each dangle piece.

2. For each short dangle, thread two gold beads onto 1" paper clip length. Use gold wire to attach medium button to dangle. Bend end of dangle to back to secure.

3. For each curled dangle, thread seventeen gold beads onto 3½" paper clip length. Use wire to attach small two-hole button to end of dangle. Bend end of dangle to back to secure. Curl button end of dangle.

4. For long dangle, thread eleven gold beads, shank button, then two gold beads onto 2½" paper clip length. Bend end of dangle to secure.

5. Straighten safety pin. Refer to Brooch with Curls Diagram, page 139, to thread beads and dangles onto safety pin close to clasp. Rebend pin to latch.

6. Use gold wire to attach large two-hole button to top of long dangle. Use gold wire to attach small shank button to clasp. Cover ends of wires on back of brooch with silicone.

EGYPTIAN SAFETY PIN BROOCH
Recycled items: two regular paper clips, fourteen 1"-long, two 1½"-long, and one 2"-long safety pins

You will also need needle-nose pliers, assorted green seed beads, gold 4mm round beads, green disc-shaped glass bead, green 15mm rectangular glass bead, clear oval-shaped glass beads, wire cutters, 26-gauge jewelry wire, and a green 8mm round glass bead.

1. Use pliers to straighten paper clips. For center dangle, form a small loop, large enough to thread onto safety pin, at one end of one paper clip.

2. (*Note:* Refer to Diagram, page 139, for Steps 2 – 7.) For center dangle, thread 25 seed beads, one gold bead, disc bead, another gold bead, rectangular bead, and three more seed beads onto paper clip; curl end of dangle to secure.

3. For dangles connecting swag, thread three seed beads and one each of the following beads onto each 1½" safety pin: gold, seed, oval, seed, gold, and seed.

4. Referring to Diagram, thread 1" safety pins with beads.

5. Use pliers to gently spread spring of 2" safety pin open, wide enough to thread dangles on pin.

6. For brooch, thread seven 1" pins according to Diagram, then one 1½" pin, onto 2" safety pin. Thread center dangle, remaining 1½" pin, then remaining 1" pins in reverse order. Gently reshape spring on pin and latch closed.

7. Secure one gold bead onto one end of a 4" length of wire. Thread wire through first pin clasp; another gold bead, and the next clasp; repeat until all seven clasps have been threaded. Secure wire around 1½" pin; trim end. Repeat for remaining side.

8. For swag, bend remaining paper clip into a U shape and thread with 28 seed beads. Bend ends through clasps of 1½" pins to secure; trim ends.

9. Use small lengths of wire (threaded with seed beads, if desired) to secure swag to dangle.

10. Making sure clasp opens and closes, carefully glue 8mm bead to 2" pin clasp.

STARBURST BUTTONS BROOCH
Recycled items: seven gold ¾"-long safety pins; one extra-large, one large, seven medium, and one small pearl button; and one large white shank button

You will also need pearl seed beads, thirteen 4mm round pearl beads, 24-gauge jewelry wire, wire cutters, needle-nose pliers, small pin back, and clear silicone adhesive.

1. Thread five seed beads onto each safety pin and latch closed.

2. Referring to Fig. 1, page 139, and alternating beads and pins, tightly thread 4mm beads and safety pins onto wire to form inner ring. Twist wire ends together to secure; trim ends.

3. Placing extra-large button at top, and referring to Fig. 2, page 139, to attach a 4mm bead to end of each safety pin except pin opposite top button, thread wire through holes in medium buttons and top of safety pins to form outer ring. Twist wire ends together to secure; trim ends.

4. For dangle, twist one end of wire through safety pin at bottom of brooch. Thread wire through large, medium, and small buttons; twist end of wire into a curl at back of small button to secure.

5. Use wire to attach shank button to inner ring; trim wire ends.

6. Glue clasp to back of extra-large button at top of brooch.

WILD ABOUT BEADS

*N*o one will ever guess that this jazzy necklace is made of items rescued from the waste basket! Create the beads using pieces cut from the rim of an aluminum baking pan and rolled-up strips from a paper bag. After painting the beads, thread them, along with ordinary wooden beads, onto a string of embroidery floss. It's the perfect necklace for casual or dressy outfits.

PAPER, METAL, AND WOODEN BEADS NECKLACE

Recycled items: disposable aluminum baking pan, paper bag, and wooden beads

You will also need utility scissors; wooden skewers; black, white, cream, tan, burgundy, and brown acrylic paint; paintbrushes; craft glue; clear acrylic spray sealer; and embroidery floss.

Rim of pan is coiled aluminum with spaces for holes. After cutting beads from rim, use a skewer to open up the "holes" in the beads; reshape ends as needed.

1. For metal beads, cut rim from pan. Cut ten ³/₈"-long beads from corners of rim; cut eight ⁵/₈"-long beads from straight edges of rim. Rub black paint onto beads to define ridges; wipe away excess paint and allow to dry.

2. For paper beads, cut three 1¹/₂" x 9¹/₄" pieces and eight 1" x 9¹/₄" pieces from paper bag. Beginning at one end and

applying a bead of glue down center of strip, roll strip tightly around skewer; glue end in place. Remove bead from skewer and allow to dry.

3. Paint animal prints on paper beads; apply two coats of sealer to beads.

4. Thread metal beads, paper beads, and wooden beads onto floss; knot ends together and trim.

PETITE LAPEL VASES

*N*ow you can take the wonderful scent of a fresh flower corsage wherever you go! Our precious lapel pins are made from tiny perfume bottles attached to safety pins. Adding a few drops of water will keep a blossom or two alive for hours. Glass leaf-shaped beads are lovely accents on these miniscule vases.

PERFUME BOTTLE LAPEL PINS

Recycled items: tiny perfume bottles

You will also need wire cutters, gold jewelry wire, 1¹/₂"-long gold safety pins, and leaf-shaped glass beads.

For each pin, wrap the center of a 10" length of wire around neck of bottle, twisting at back to secure. Pulling pin as close to bottle as possible, wrap wire ends tightly around non-opening side of pin to ends of pin; trim ends. Wrap the center of a 4" length of wire around neck of bottle and twist twice at front to secure. Thread one bead onto each end of wire; make a tight curl in wire end at desired length and trim.

FUN FIX-UPS

*d*iscover treasures in your trash that give a whole new meaning to creative recycling! Fashion a whimsical dog-shaped catch game using a juice can, or a precious powder box doll chair decorated with dainty fabric and ruffles. Create handmade soaps in assorted containers, or mix chunks of old candles to create colorful new ones. From handy organizers to unique home accents, you won't believe what wonders are waiting in your wastebasket!

DARLING DOLL CHAIR

*A*ny little girl will love playing with this adorable doll chair! Two powder boxes decorated with fabric scraps are stacked on top of each other to create hidden storage spaces for doll shoes and other tiny accessories. The elegant back is crafted from a cardboard mailing tube, and assorted buttons and trims provide cute accents for this perfectly precious furniture piece.

POWDER BOX DOLL CHAIR

Recycled items: two identical cardboard powder boxes with lids (we used 1⁵/₈"h x 3¹/₄" dia. boxes), fabric scraps, heavy-weight cardboard, nail, assorted small buttons, assorted trims, heavy-weight cardboard mailing tube piece (we used a 6"h x 3" dia. tube piece), poster board, and polyester fiberfill

You will also need spray adhesive, hot glue gun, high-loft batting, cotton batting, craft glue, long upholstery needle, heavy-duty thread, tracing paper, and heavy-duty utility scissors.

Use craft glue for all gluing unless otherwise indicated; allow to dry after each application.

1. Remove lid from one box. Measure height and circumference of lid, then cut a strip of fabric the determined measurements. Use spray adhesive to glue strip around lid.

2. For pleated skirt, multiply each measurement in Step 1 by two; add ¹/₂" to height and 2" to circumference. Cut a piece of fabric the determined measurements; press one short edge ¹/₂" to wrong side. Matching wrong sides, press fabric in half lengthwise. Beginning with raw end and forming pleats as you go, hot glue raw edges of fabric along lower edge of box lid.

3. For seat cushion, draw around top of lid once on cardboard and five times on high-loft batting; cut out circles. Use nail to punch a small hole at center of circle. Draw around cardboard circle once on cotton batting; cut out ¹/₄" outside drawn line. Draw around cardboard circle on wrong side of fabric; cut out 2" outside drawn line.

4. Press edge of fabric circle ¹/₄" to wrong side; work *Running Stitches*, page 158, along folded edge. Place cotton batting circle, high-loft batting circles, then cardboard circle at center of fabric circle; pull ends of thread to tightly gather fabric over cardboard circle. Knot thread ends. Glue cushion to lid. Using long needle and heavy-duty thread and stitching through all layers, sew buttons to center top and bottom of seat.

5. Glue first box bottom to top of remaining powder box; place fabric-covered lid on stacked boxes.

6. Cut a strip of fabric 2"w by the circumference of the boxes. Press strip in half lengthwise; unfold. Press long raw edges of strip to center; fold in half lengthwise. Covering raw edges of fabrics, glue strip along edges where fabrics join. Hot glue a length of trim along line where cushion joins box lid.

7. Trace chairback pattern, page 145, onto tracing paper; cut out. Draw around pattern on mailing tube, poster board, and cotton batting; cut out along drawn lines. Draw around pattern on wrong sides of two different fabrics; cut out ¹/₂" outside drawn lines.

8. Use spray adhesive to adhere batting shape to inside surface of mailing tube shape; repeat with one fabric piece, gluing raw edges to back of mailing tube shape. Repeat to cover poster board shape with remaining fabric shape. Glue covered poster board shape to back of mailing tube shape to complete chairback. Hot glue trim along all edges of chairback.

9. Place chairback on seat; mark position for buttons on lower front corners of chairback and at same position on sides of seat just above fabric strip. Remove chairback; use nail to punch two holes ¹/₈" apart on each side of each mark. Apply glue along inner back edge of chairback; replace chairback on seat. Working through holes, sew buttons to chair.

10. For pillow, cut a 5¹/₂" dia. circle of fabric. Press edge of circle ¹/₄" to wrong side; work *Running Stitches* along folded edge. Place fiberfill at center of circle; pull ends of thread to tightly gather circle over fiberfill. Knot thread ends. Stitching through pillow, sew buttons to center front and center back of pillow.

LITTLE GIRL'S KEEPSAKE BOX

*L*ittle girls collect lots of treasures and need a place to store those special odds and ends. This cute keepsake chest is simply a shoebox covered with fabric. Flower buttons and a coordinating fleece butterfly on the padded lid give the box an extra-feminine finishing touch.

GIRL'S KEEPSAKE SHOEBOX

Recycled item: a cardboard shoebox with side-hinged lid

You will also need a knife with a thin blade, two coordinating fabrics, polyester high-loft batting, hot glue gun, $1/2$"w paper-backed fusible web tape, craft glue, tracing paper, pink polyester fleece, and seven flower-shaped shank buttons with shanks removed.

Use craft glue for all gluing unless otherwise indicated.

1. Using knife as necessary to open glued seams, carefully unfold box. To cover outside of box, place one fabric, wrong side up, on flat surface; place unfolded box, outside down, at center of fabric. Draw around box on fabric; cut out shape 3" outside drawn lines.

2. Cut pieces from batting to fit top and sides of lid; glue pieces in place. Overlapping to inside, glue fabric to box.

3. For inside liner, place remaining fabric wrong side up on flat surface. Place box, inside down, at center of fabric. Draw around box on fabric; cut out $1/2$" outside drawn lines. For hem, follow tape manufacturer's instructions to make a $1/2$"w hem in edges of fabric. Glue liner to inside of box.

4. Reassemble box, hot gluing to secure.

5. Trace butterfly pattern, page 145, onto tracing paper; cut out. Use pattern to cut butterfly from fleece. Glue butterfly to top of lid.

6. Hot glue three buttons along front edge of box; hot glue remaining buttons to butterfly.

CANINE CATCH GAME

*Y*ou won't need a partner to play catch when you make this entertaining toy! Transform a cardboard juice can into the canine "catcher" with a craft foam face, tongue, and big floppy ears. A dowel attached to the can provides a handle, and a small rubber ball connected to a piece of string completes the game.

DOG CAN CATCH GAME

Recycled items: 2⅝" dia. x 5"h cardboard can (we used an orange juice concentrate can), small wood screw, 20" of string, and a small rubber ball

You will also need light pink acrylic paint; paintbrushes; drill and bits; 3" of ⅝" dia. dowel; brown, tan, red, black, and white craft foam sheets; hot glue gun; tracing paper; hole punch; and a large-eye embroidery needle.

1. Paint inside of can light pink; allow to dry.

2. Drill a small pilot hole at center in end of can and at one end of dowel. Inserting screw from inside of can, use screw to attach dowel to outside of can for handle.

3. Measure circumference and height of can; cut a piece of brown foam the determined measurements. With seam at bottom, glue piece around can.

4. Trace patterns, pages 146 and 147, onto tracing paper; cut out. Use patterns to cut one muzzle from tan foam; one tongue from red foam; one nose and two pupils from black foam; one head, one head bottom, and two ears from brown foam; and two eyes from white foam. Punch eight whisker freckles from brown foam.

5. Glue head bottom to bottom of can; with flat end of muzzle even with sealed end of can, center and glue muzzle to top of can. Overlapping muzzle about 1½", glue head to muzzle; glue ears to head. Glue tongue in open end of can. Glue nose and freckles to muzzle; glue eyes to head and pupils to eyes.

6. Thread string through needle; thread needle through center of ball. Tie one end of string into a knot close to ball and remaining end around handle close to can; glue knots to secure.

MOSAIC NOTES

*F*or a truly memorable gift, brighten someone's day with a "heartfelt" collection of coordinating cards. Create our mosaic design from colorful pieces of old greeting cards, then photocopy the design onto blank note cards. "Frame" the original mosaic in the box lid and embellish with buttons and hand-drawn "stitches."

FRAMED MOSAIC CARD SET

Recycled items: a cardboard box with lid to accommodate note cards and envelopes (our box measures 6½" x 9"), clear plastic take-out food container lid, greeting cards, and four buttons

You will also need utility scissors, red spray paint, hot glue gun, white card stock, tracing paper, black permanent fine-point marker, blank note cards and envelopes, decorative-edge craft scissors, and tissue paper.

1. Draw, then cut out a 3½" x 5¾" opening for window at center of box lid. Paint box and lid red; allow to dry.

2. Cut a 5" x 7" piece of plastic for "glass"; glue in place behind window in lid.

3. Measure inside length and width of lid; for insert, cut a piece of white card stock the determined measurements. Draw a 4" x 6" rectangle at center of insert.

4. Trace heart patterns, page 148, onto tracing paper; cut out. Using patterns, cut four heart shapes from greeting cards; arrange and glue hearts within drawn rectangle on insert. Cut pieces from cards to fill in around hearts; glue pieces in place on insert to complete mosaic design.

5. Use marker to draw "stitches" along edges of hearts and window. Glue one button at each corner of window.

6. Photocopy mosaic design onto blank note cards. Center and glue insert with original mosaic design behind window.

7. For tab, cut two hearts from greeting cards, using craft scissors to cut out large heart; glue small heart to large heart. Cut a piece of tissue paper for box liner. Place liner, then cards and envelopes, in box; fold ends of liner over card set, and glue top of tab to top flap of liner.

SASSY SALSA SERVING MAT

*A*dd pizzazz to your next fiesta with this sassy serving mat. Using the back of a piece of vinyl floor covering as your "canvas," simply transfer the pattern and fill it in with paint. Bright colors make the mat a zesty addition to your party table settings.

VINYL SERVING MAT

Recycled item: a piece of vinyl floor covering (we used a 12" x 17" piece)

You will also need white gesso, assorted colors of acrylic paint, paintbrushes, stylus, transfer paper, black permanent

medium-point marker, clear acrylic spray sealer, and utility scissors.

Allow gesso, paint, and sealer to dry after each application.

1. Enlarge salsa pattern, page 155, to desired size for mat.

2. Apply two coats of gesso, then basecoat color, to wrong side of vinyl. Using stylus and transfer paper, transfer pattern to center of vinyl.

3. Paint design. Apply two coats of sealer to mat. Use marker to outline designs.

4. Use utility scissors to cut out mat 3/4" outside edges of design. If desired, paint edges of mat and apply sealer.

EASY PETITE SOAPS

*H*ere's a great gift idea that really comes in handy for the kitchen or bathroom. Round up an assortment of "molds" recycled from disposable items such as pudding cups and plastic bottle bottoms. Drop pieces of pre-colored soaps into the molds, then fill with melted soap and let harden. These glycerin soaps are so easy and inexpensive to make, you can craft enough to share with everyone!

HANDMADE SOAPS

Recycled items: containers for molds (we used petit four papers, plastic cookie tray, pudding cups, and the bottom of a plastic beverage bottle)

You will also need mold release spray; pre-colored crafting soap, clear glycerin soap bricks, soap dye, and soap fragrance.

Follow Steps 1, 3, and 4 to make single-color soaps or your own "pre-colored soaps" for Step 2. Follow all steps for multi-color soaps.

1. For molds, cut desired portions from recycled containers; apply mold release to inside of containers.

2. Cut pieces from pre-colored soaps and arrange in containers as desired.

3. Following manufacturer's instructions, melt glycerin soap brick; add dye and fragrance to melted soap as desired.

4. Pour melted soap into molds; allow to harden, then remove from molds.

BLOOMING PINCUSHION

*Y*ou don't have to worry about those loose pins on your sewing table anymore! Our crafty pincushion is not only handy, it makes use of items you might otherwise discard. A plastic cap from a detergent bottle is transformed into a pincushion when hosiery is stuffed inside. Brightly colored wired ribbon and artificial flowers add pretty finishing touches to this economical project.

DETERGENT CAP PINCUSHION

Recycled items: artificial flowers, cap from liquid detergent bottle, and hosiery

You will also need a hot glue gun and 1¹/₂"w wire-edged ribbon.

1. Leaving one flower intact, remove leaves and petals from flowers.

2. Glue leaves, then petals around outside rim of detergent cap.

3. Measure around rim of cap and add 1"; cut a length of ribbon the determined measurement. Fold one end of ribbon ¹/₂" to wrong side. Overlapping folded end over raw end and covering ends of petals, glue one edge (bottom edge) of ribbon around rim of cap.

4. Stuff hosiery into cap.

5. Pull ends of wire to gather top edge of ribbon over hosiery; bend wire ends to secure, then trim excess wire.

6. Glue remaining flower to top of pincushion.

RIBBON CADDY

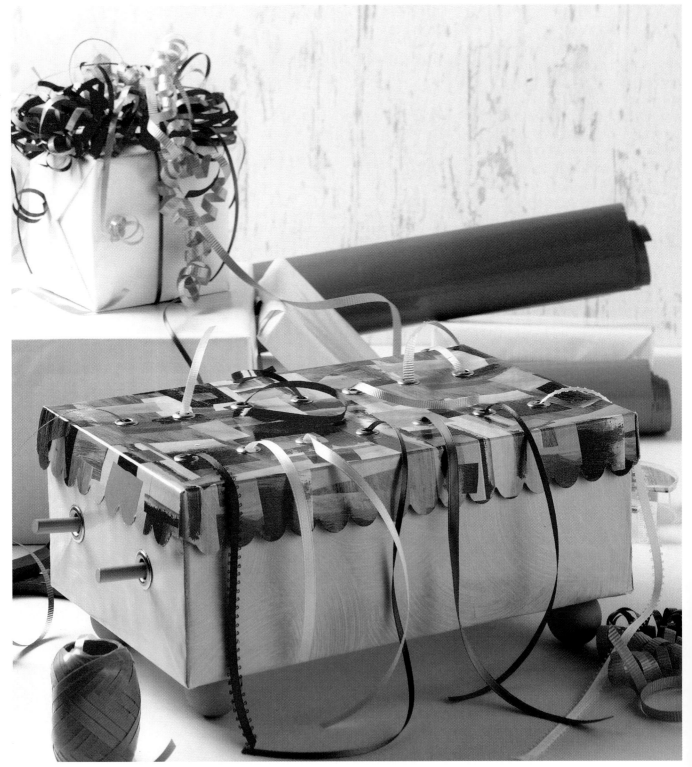

*D*on't fight that tangled mess *of ribbon anymore — keep your collection neat and accessible with our nifty caddy! A wrapping paper-covered shoebox is ideal for holding spools of ribbon on wooden dowels. Grommet holes in the box keep each spool flowing separately, eliminating the hassle of intertwined ribbon.*

SHOEBOX RIBBON CADDY

Recycled items: a shoebox with lid, wide enough to accommodate two side by side rows of ribbon spools that are $3^1/_4$" dia. or smaller (we used a 7" x $11^1/_2$" box); and two coordinating wrapping papers

You will also need spray adhesive, hot glue gun, assorted spools of ribbon including two $3^1/_4$" dia. spools, $5/_8$" dia. and $1/_4$" dia. metal grommets, saw, $5/_8$" dia. dowel, acrylic paint, paintbrushes, four $1^1/_2$" dia. wooden ball knobs for feet, and decorative-edge craft scissors.

1. Carefully disassemble box. Cut a piece of paper 1" larger on all sides than unfolded box. Place paper, right side down, on a flat surface. Apply spray adhesive to outside of box. Center unfolded box, adhesive side down, on paper; press firmly to secure.

2. Trim paper $1/_2$" outside edges of box; clip into corners diagonally and glue edges to inside of box. Reassemble box.

3. To mark placement for grommets, evenly space two $3^1/_4$" dia. spools, side by side, on end of box and mark center holes. Follow manufacturer's instructions to attach $5/_8$" dia. grommets at marks. Repeat for opposite end of box.

4. For each spool holder, measure length of box and add 2"; cut a piece of dowel the determined measurement. Paint spool holder and allow to dry. Thread spools of ribbon onto holder; thread ends of holder through grommets.

5. Paint feet and allow to dry; glue to bottom of box.

6. Using remaining paper, repeat Step 1 to cover box lid. Use craft scissors to trim edges of lid.

7. Spacing evenly, follow manufacturer's instructions to attach one $1/_4$" dia. grommet for each spool of ribbon to lid; reassemble lid.

8. Thread ends of ribbons through grommets in lid; place lid on box.

RESOURCEFUL TIEBACKS

Transform brown paper bags into fun, decorative accessories in no time at all! Our resourceful curtain tiebacks are simply strips of painted brown paper folded and linked into a geometric design. Buttons make for clever trims, and pieces of a wire coat hanger hold the tieback around the curtain.

PAPER BAG CHAIN TIEBACKS

Recycled items: brown paper bags, clothes hanger, and large buttons

You will also need fabric tape measure, brown acrylic paint, paintbrush, hot glue gun, pliers, and two cup hooks.

1. Loosely wrap a tape measure around gathered curtain at desired height for tieback; cut a length of clothes hanger the determined measurement. Use half of the determined measurement for length of tieback.

2. Lightly *Dry Brush*, page 157, several bags with brown paint for one half of links and locks; *Dry Brush* several other bags with a heavier coverage of brown paint for remaining half of links and locks. Allow to dry.

3. For each link of one tieback, cut a 4" x 143/4" piece from painted paper bag; cut an equal number of links from light and dark painted bags for desired length of tieback.

4. For each paper piece, fold long edges 1/4" to unpainted side; matching long edges, fold in half lengthwise. Matching ends, fold in half, then unfold; fold ends to center fold, then refold.

5. Referring to Fig. 1, and alternating color of links, join links together to form a chain.

Fig. 1

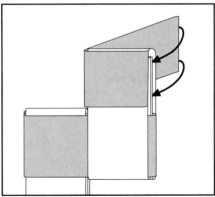

6. For locks, cut two 4" x 73/8" pieces from opposite color bag than beginning link. Follow Step 3 to fold locks.

7. To secure chain, insert one lock in last link. Unfold ends of remaining lock. Wrap lock around beginning link and tuck ends between folds in link (Fig. 2).

Fig. 2

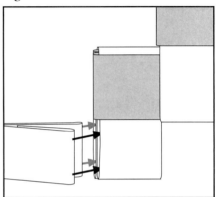

8. Glue one button to each top "square" in tieback.

9. To attach tieback to curtain, thread hanger wire length through back of tieback; use pliers to make a small hook in each end of wire. Wrapping wire around curtain, arrange tieback on curtain; interlock hooks together at back of curtain to secure.

10. To attach tieback to wall, screw one cup hook into wall at desired placement; slip wire on tieback over cup hook.

CHUNKY CANDLES

*W*hen your old candles have
seen better days, revive them with
this resourceful "recycling" project!
Using ice-cream and juice cartons as
molds, simply fill them with large or
small chunks of old candles and pour
in melted clear wax. The ice-cream
carton lid provides a base for one
of the colorful wax creations and
iridescent wire-edged ribbon
accents both.

CANDLES FROM CANDLES

Recycled items: candles, ice-cream
carton with lid, and a beverage carton

You will also need wired candle wicks,
clear candle wax, hot glue gun, 1"w ribbon,
decorative cord, and wired ribbons.

1. Cut candles into large chunks; separate
chunks from smaller pieces.

2. Positioning wicks, fill ice-cream carton
with large chunks and beverage carton
with remaining smaller pieces. Following
Working With Wax, page 158, melt clear
wax and pour into cartons; allow to
harden. Tear cartons away from candles.

3. For ice-cream carton candle base, glue
1"w ribbon around ice-cream carton lid,
gluing ribbon edges over rim. Glue cord
along edge of lid; place candle on base.

4. Knot a length of wired ribbon around
each candle.

NATURAL MASTERPIECE

*R*escue those miscellaneous
paper items from the trash
and transform them into this
magnificent "recycled" masterpiece!
Our nature-inspired wall art is two
projects in one — the frame is
created from layered strips of
corrugated cardboard, and the
handmade paper design is fashioned
from egg carton pulp and dried
flower stems. Because you can press
almost anything into your paper, the
creative possibilities are endless!

FRAMED HANDMADE PAPER

Recycled items: heavy-weight cardboard
(we used the back of a writing tablet),
corrugated cardboard, paper egg carton
(we used a yellow carton), dried floral
stems, and a brown paper bag

You will also need craft glue; brown,
dark green, and light green acrylic paint;
paintbrushes; clear acrylic spray sealer;
and a self-adhesive picture hanger.

*Allow glue, paint, and sealer to dry after
each application.*

1. For backing, cut a 10$^1/_2$" square from
heavy-weight cardboard. For frame, cut
the following size strips from corrugated
cardboard: four 1$^1/_2$" x 10", two 1" x 10",
two 1" x 9$^1/_2$", two $^1/_2$" x 9$^1/_2$", and two
$^1/_2$" x 9".

2. Working from largest to smallest,
centering strips, and overlapping corners,
stack and glue cardboard strips on
backing to form frame.

3. Paint backing inside frame brown.
Follow *Dry Brush*, page 157, to paint
frame with brown, dark green, then light
green paint. Apply sealer to frame.

4. For handmade paper, use egg carton
and follow *Paper Making*, page 159, to
make paper pulp. Roll wet pulp to desired
size and thickness, placing dried stems on
top of pulp during the rolling process;
allow to dry flat. If necessary, tear edges
of paper piece to fit in frame.

5. Tear a piece from paper bag about the
same size as handmade paper; crumple,
then smooth out paper piece. Glue brown
paper, then handmade paper in frame.

6. Attach hanger to back of frame.

SHUTTER-TOP TABLE

Wouldn't it be nice to have another spot to display your special treasures? This inventive table is perfect for placing in a hallway or behind the sofa, and it's made with items you might otherwise throw away! An old wooden shutter provides a top for the table, and cardboard mailing tubes make attractive legs when covered with fabric.

SHUTTER AND MAILING TUBES TABLE

Recycled items: a wooden shutter (we used a 13" x 36" shutter), three wooden yardsticks (we used 1⁵⁄₈"w yardsticks), and four heavy-duty mailing tubes with end caps (we used 3¹⁄₄" dia. mailing tubes with center holes in end caps)

You will also need spray primer, light green and dark green acrylic paint, paintbrushes, saw, hot glue gun, two coordinating green fabrics, four wood screws, four washers (larger in diameter than holes in tube end caps and with center holes smaller than screw heads), drill and bits, spray adhesive, ⁵⁄₈" dia. dowel, and glass to fit shutter.

Refer to Table Assembly Diagram, page 139, for assembling table. Allow primer and paint to dry after each application.

To determine length of wood screws needed, measure total thickness of cap, washer, and shutter and subtract ¹⁄₄". Drill pilot holes before inserting screws.

1. For tabletop, apply primer, then light green paint to shutter.

2. For apron, measure length of shutter and subtract 2"; cut two pieces of yardstick the determined measurement. Measure width of shutter and subtract 2"; cut two pieces of yardstick the determined measurement. Glue apron pieces to wrong side of shutter.

3. Measure around apron; add ¹⁄₂". Measure height of apron; multiply by 2. Cut a strip of fabric the determined measurements. Beginning ¹⁄₂" past one corner and matching one long edge of fabric to top outside edge of apron, glue fabric strip around apron. Wrap and glue bottom edge of fabric over apron edge to inside of apron.

4. Remove caps from ends of tubes. Using screws and washers, refer to Fig. 1 to attach one end cap from each tube to tabletop inside each apron corner.

Fig. 1

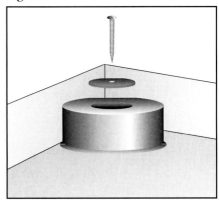

5. Cut mailing tubes to desired height for table legs. Drill a ⁵⁄₈" dia. hole 1⁴" from top in each leg for crossbar support.

6. To cover each leg, measure height of tube; add 2". Measure around leg; add 1". Cut a piece of remaining fabric the determined measurements. Apply spray adhesive to wrong side of fabric; center and smooth fabric around tube. Fold fabric to inside at each end of tube. Cut an X through fabric over support hole. Place remaining end cap in bottom of leg.

7. For crossbar supports, measure distance between outside edges of end caps on short ends of tabletop; subtract ¹⁄₂". Cut two pieces of dowel the determined measurement. Paint supports dark green.

8. Glue one support in holes between each pair of legs; glue legs to end caps on underside of tabletop.

9. Mitering corners, glue strips of fabric along inner edges on top of tabletop. Place glass on tabletop.

CREATIVE CELEBRATIONS

Celebrate in style with these fun decorations and party accessories. Pep up a child's birthday gathering with colorful treat totes made from plastic frosting containers and cute candy-tube necklaces filled with bubble solution. Get patriotic with a star-spangled picnic caddy or add sparkle to the Christmas season with ornaments fashioned from old jewelry. Whatever the occasion, you can make it merrier with these clever "recycled" crafts!

B-A-B-Y BLOCKS

*H*ere's a sweet way to decorate your party table at a baby shower ... or brighten the little one's room after the celebration. Rescue cardboard beverage cartons from the trash and use them to make four blocks to stack and spell B-A-B-Y. Cover the blocks with pieces of receiving blanket, add felt squares and letters, and trim the blocks with baby rickrack and novelty buttons.

Recycled items: half-gallon cardboard beverage cartons and a baby receiving blanket

You will also need a hot glue gun, assorted felt, baby rickrack, tracing paper, pliers, and assorted baby-motif shank buttons.

CARTON BABY BLOCK CENTERPIECE

1. For each block, draw lines around one carton 7³/₄" and 3⁷/₈" from bottom edge. Cut top from carton along 7³/₄" line. Cut down each corner of carton to 3⁷/₈" line. Fold sections in and glue in place to make block.

2. Cut an 8¹/₂" x 16¹/₂" piece from receiving blanket. Use blanket piece to wrap block gift-wrap style; glue to secure.

3. Cut two 3³/₄" squares of felt; glue onto opposite sides of block covering folded blanket edges.

4. Repeat Steps 1 – 3 to make three more blocks.

5. Glue a 14¹/₄" length of rickrack along edges of each felt square. Trace letter patterns, page 149, onto tracing paper; cut out. Using patterns, cut four B's, two A's, and two Y's from felt. Center and glue letters to blocks over felt. Use pliers to remove shanks from buttons; glue buttons to blocks.

CREATIVE GIFT CARRIER

*P*ut a new twist on gift giving with this inventive carrier! Simply find two cardboard boxes that fit together, add handles, and cover with wallpaper scraps. Almost a gift in itself, this creative tote can be made in any size you need.

GIFT BOX WITH HANDLES

Recycled items: two boxes that fit together for bottom and lid (we used a laundry detergent box and a saltine cracker box), handles from old gift bag, scraps of wallpaper and wallpaper border, and ribbon

You will also need spray primer, craft glue, foam brush (optional), and a craft knife and cutting mat.

If desired, use foam brush to apply glue to box. Allow glue to dry after each application.

1. For gift box, cut top from detergent box and discard. For gift box lid, cut remaining box to fit over top of gift box.

2. Apply primer to box and lid; allow to dry.

3. Glue handles to inside top of box. Cut a slot in top of lid for each handle.

4. Folding and gluing edges of paper to inside top of box and wrapping bottom of box gift-wrap style, cover gift box with wallpaper. Cover lid with wallpaper.

Working from inside of lid, use craft knife to cut paper from slots for handles.

5. Overlapping $1/2$" at back, glue wallpaper border around lid. Tie ribbon into a bow; glue to front of lid.

PRECIOUS HANDS MAGNETS

*W*ant a handy idea for using
large sheet magnets after their
printed advertising becomes dated?
Our precious magnets are not only
sentimental keepsakes, but they also
come in handy for posting notes,
lists, or pictures. Just cover the
magnet with decorative paper and
cut it out in the shape of a child's
hand. Personalize it with the child's
name and heart-shaped photo.

KIDS' HANDS MAGNETS

Recycled items: large advertiser's sheet
magnets and a photograph

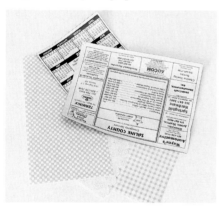

You will also need self-adhesive
decorative paper, tracing paper, craft
glue stick, and a black permanent fine-
point marker.

1. For each magnet, apply decorative
paper to front of magnet.

2. Draw around child's hand on magnet;
cut out along drawn lines.

3. Trace heart pattern, page 148, onto
tracing paper; cut out. Draw around
pattern over desired area of photograph;
cut out. Glue photograph to magnet.

4. Use marker to write child's name
on magnet.

FUN PARTY PACKS

*S*end your party guests home with fanciful containers filled to the rim with yummy treats! Plastic containers from ready-to-spread frosting become charming goody totes when decorated with card stock labels colorfully embellished with each guest's name. Ribbon loops make ornamental trimmings as well as convenient handles for carrying these delightful totes.

FROSTING CONTAINER TREAT HOLDERS

Recycled items: plastic frosting containers with lids

For each container, you will also need assorted colors of card stock, decorative-edge craft scissors, black permanent fine-point marker, craft glue stick, awl, $^3/_8$"w ribbon, $^1/_2$" dia. wooden bead, pony bead, and a hot glue gun.

Use craft glue stick for all gluing unless otherwise indicated.

1. For each treat holder, measure height, then circumference of container; cut out background from card stock the determined measurements. Use craft scissors to cut out two $^1/_2$"w strips from contrasting card stock the circumference measurement.

2. Use marker to draw desired designs on strips.

3. Glue background around container; glue strips along top and bottom edges of background.

4. For letters, enlarge alphabet patterns, page 150, 150% on photocopier and print onto card stock; cut out letters and glue to background.

5. For handle, use awl to punch a small hole at center of lid. Thread both ends of a 10" length of ribbon through wooden bead, through hole in lid, and through pony bead; knot ribbon ends together on inside of lid. Pull handle until pony bead is snug between knot in ribbon and lid; hot glue bottom of wooden bead to lid.

PEGGY SUE PARTY PURSE

*S*ure to be the hit of a little girl's party, our tiny tin box purse is as easy to make as it is fun to give! We simply painted a "doll" face on a breath mint container, then added bright yarn pigtails. A piece of rattail cord gives this precious purse a handle for easy carrying.

TIN BOX PARTY FAVOR

Recycled items: a small hinged metal tin and a 10" square of cardboard

You will also need a hammer and nail; spray primer; flesh, blue, red, and pink acrylic paint; paintbrushes; tracing paper; transfer paper; black permanent fine-point marker; clear acrylic spray sealer; 8" of rattail cord; hot glue gun; yarn; and $1/16$"w satin ribbon.

Allow primer, paint, and sealer to dry after each application.

1. For handle, use hammer and nail to punch two holes 2" apart at center of hinged side of tin.

2. Apply primer, then flesh paint to tin.

3. Trace face pattern, page 148, onto tracing paper. Use transfer paper to transfer design to lid of tin. Use marker to draw over transferred lines. Paint eyes blue, lips red, and cheeks pink.

4. Apply two coats sealer to tin.

5. For handle, thread ends of cord through holes in tin; knot ends and glue to secure.

6. For hair, wrap yarn around cardboard twenty times. Tie a 6" length of yarn around hair at one edge of cardboard; cut yarn along opposite edge of cardboard. Braid each section of hair; use a 5" length of ribbon to secure each braid. Glue hair along edges of tin.

BUBBLY BAUBLE

Have a "bubbly" good time anywhere with our entertaining necklace! Use a sticker-covered candy container tied with plastic lacing to create this inventive bauble. Sparkling beads threaded onto craft wire form a fancy wand for dipping into the bubble solution.

CANDY CONTAINER BUBBLE NECKLACE

Recycled items: small plastic candy container with lid (we used a mini milk chocolate candy container) and assorted beads (we used pony and pebble beads)

You will also need self-adhesive stickers, 36" of plastic lacing, hot glue gun, 12" of 24-gauge plastic-coated craft wire, and liquid dish detergent.

1. Apply stickers to container.

2. For necklace, knot center of lacing around container hinge; apply a drop of glue to knot to secure. Knot lacing ends together; apply a drop of glue to knot to secure.

3. For wand, form a circle at one end of wire small enough to fit in container for bubble-blowing loop; twist wire end around wire to secure. Thread beads onto remaining end of wire; form another small circle for handle, thread wire back through beads, then twist wire under handle to secure.

4. For bubble mixture, mix one part dish detergent with two parts water. Pour mixture into container; place wand in container and close lid.

Hand out sweet sentiments to all your party guests with these heart-shaped, candy-filled valentines! Simply sew hearts cut from cereal box liners onto construction paper to create "pouches" for holding tiny treats. Tie up the openings with ribbon bows for a precious finish.

VALENTINE PARTY FAVORS

Recycled items: clear plastic liners from cereal boxes and construction paper

You will also need decorative-edge craft scissors, removable tape, $1/8$" dia. hole punch, candies, and $1/8$"w satin ribbon.

1. For each party favor, cut liner open along bottom edge, then use a cool iron to press liner flat.

2. Trace heart pattern, page 148, onto liner; use craft scissors to cut out heart along drawn lines.

3. Tape heart to construction paper. Using a $1/4$" seam allowance and leaving a 1"w opening at top of heart, sew heart to construction paper. Remove tape. Use craft scissors to cut out construction paper $3/4$" outside sewn lines.

4. Punch one hole at each end of opening in heart. Fill favor with candies. Thread a 10" length of ribbon through holes and tie into a bow at front of favor to secure candies in place.

FAIRY-TALE PRINCE

You may think frog princes only exist in fairy tales, but this royal "ribbitter" can be brought to life in no time! Use a paper egg carton to craft his crouching body and pointed crown, then top the points with old beads. Metallic paints and iridescent button eyes give this prince his sparkling personality.

EGG CARTON FROG PRINCE

Recycled items: paper egg carton, four small beads for crown, and two shank buttons for eyes (we used antique buttons with metal shanks)

You will also need tracing paper; utility scissors; hot glue gun; white spray primer; metallic green, orange, light green, and metallic gold acrylic paint; paintbrushes; clear glossy acrylic spray sealer; and awl.

Allow primer, paint, and sealer to dry after each application.

1. Trace frog patterns, page 151, onto tracing paper; cut out. Use patterns to cut hind legs with feet (cut two, one in reverse), front feet (cut two, one in reverse), and lips from egg carton. Referring to Fig. 1, cut egg cups for body (including arcs for mouth opening) and crown.

Fig. 1

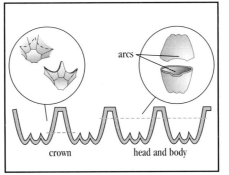

2. Referring to Frog Assembly Diagram, page 140, glue cup sections together to form body. Carefully bend hind legs to form "knees" and "ankles." Glue ankles to ends of legs; glue legs to body. Glue front feet to body. Glue lips along arcs of mouth opening. Glue one bead to each crown point.

3. Apply primer to frog and crown. Paint frog metallic green, inner edges of mouth orange, lips and chest light green, and crown gold. Paint light green dots on back and legs of frog.

4. Glue crown to head. Apply two coats of sealer to frog.

5. For eyes, use awl to punch small holes in head to insert shanks of buttons; glue buttons to head.

ORNAMENTAL EGG TREE

A beautiful addition to your Easter décor, our lovely tree is an "egg-ceptional" way to welcome everyone's favorite spring holiday. Create the realistic tree by using plaster to anchor branches into a rusted coffee can. Plan ahead to collect the eggshells when cooking with eggs, carefully emptying the shells as directed in Step 3. Fashion the intricate ornaments by gluing leaves and flowers to the eggshells before dipping into a strong coffee bath. Paint-pen accents brighten the relief designs left on the dyed eggshells, and loops of raffia provide hangers for the ornaments.

DECORATED EGG TREE

Recycled items: large rusted can (we used a coffee can), branches (we used a small bare branch and two berry branches), white and brown eggs, large clean jar with lid, small leaves and flowers, hosiery, and string

You will also need plaster of Paris, wire cutters, rusted craft wire, long thin needle, rubber gloves, chlorine bleach, paper towels, craft glue stick, instant coffee, metallic paint pens, raffia, craft glue, and wood excelsior.

Use craft glue for all gluing unless otherwise indicated.

1. For base, follow manufacturer's instructions to mix plaster. Pour plaster into can to within 1" from top and let set briefly; insert branches. Allow to harden completely.

2. Cut varying lengths of wire. Curl wire lengths around branches. To fill in bare spots, curl additional wire lengths around branches leaving 6" to 8" tails; wrap tails around a pencil to form tendrils.

3. For each egg, use long needle to punch a hole in both ends of egg, breaking yolk. With egg over a bowl, blow into one end of egg to empty contents from shell.

4. (*Caution*: Wear rubber gloves and work in a well-ventilated area when working with bleach.) Thoroughly rinse eggshells in water. Place eggshells in a jar and cover with one part bleach to one part water. Place lid on jar and allow eggshells to soak 24 hours. Remove eggshells from jar and place on several layers of paper towels to dry.

5. For each egg with leaf and flower designs, use glue stick to adhere leaves and flowers to a white eggshell, making sure all edges are glued down. Stretch hosiery over eggshell, gathering edges at top of eggshell. Tie string around gathers; trim excess hosiery.

6. For dye bath, make four cups of strong coffee. Submerge covered eggs in coffee until filled; allow to set until desired color is achieved, checking and turning eggs for even coverage. Remove eggs from coffee, drain, and pat dry; carefully remove hosiery, leaves, and flowers.

7. To decorate all eggs, use paint pens to add details and to outline edges of shapes on eggs and allow to dry.

8. Making a small knot, knot ends of a 10" length of raffia together to form a loop for each hanger. Using craft glue, glue knot into top hole in egg; allow to dry.

9. Tie several lengths of raffia into a bow around base. Cover plaster with excelsior. Hang eggs on tree.

SPRINGTIME WREATH

A few moments spent sorting through your recycling bin will turn up almost everything you need to fashion this plush springtime wreath! Shape a wire coat hanger into a circle and tie on bundles of strips cut from white plastic bags. Embellish with yellow plastic bag flowers and painted leaves and a banner cut from foam trays. A bit of pastel ribbon finishes this oh-so-fresh decoration.

PLASTIC BAGS WREATH

Recycled items: a wire coat hanger, white and yellow plastic bags, plastic foam trays, and twist ties

You will also need pliers, tracing paper, stylus, green floral spray paint, black permanent marker, low-temperature glue gun, and 1½"w ribbon.

1. Use pliers to shape hanger into a circle and to form hook into a hanger loop.

2. Cut white bags into 1" x 8" strips. Layering three strips into a bundle, tie bundles around hanger wire until circle is thickly covered to make wreath.

3. Trace patterns, page 151, onto tracing paper; cut out. Use patterns to cut one banner, four small leaves, and four large leaves from foam trays. Use a stylus to emboss veins on leaves. Spray paint banner and leaves green; allow to dry. Use marker to write message on banner.

4. For each flower, fold one yellow bag lengthwise to measure a 3" wide strip. Refer to Fig. 1 to fold and roll strip to form flower center. Continue rolling strip around flower center, winding upwards slightly and gluing in place as you go (pushing bag up with your thumb and spot gluing between layers helps shape petals); secure bottom of flower center with twist tie.

Fig. 1

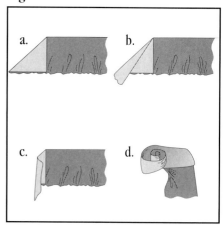

5. Arrange and glue flowers, ribbon, leaves, and banner to wreath.

DARLING BUNNY BASKET

Get things hopping this Easter with an adorable bunny basket! Fashioned from one-gallon bleach bottles, this fun project will delight little ones. Pretty springtime ribbon adds splashes of color to each bunny as well as to the buttoned-on handle.

BLEACH BOTTLE BUNNY BASKET

Recycled items: two 1-gallon bleach bottles and two buttons

You will also need tracing paper, utility scissors, stylus, transfer paper, pink paint pen, black permanent marker, hot glue gun, $^3/_8$"w ribbon, ice pick, and heavy-duty thread.

1. Trace bunny pattern, page 152, onto tracing paper; cut out.

2. Use a pencil to lightly draw lines around one bottle 7" and $3^1/_4$" from bottle bottom; cut top from bottle along the 7" line. Mark placement for handle ends on opposite sides of bottle at $3^1/_4$" line.

3. Placing lower edge of pattern on drawn line, use pattern to lightly draw two evenly spaced bunny heads on each side of bottle between marks for handle ends; cut out.

4. Use stylus and transfer paper to transfer face pattern onto each bunny. Paint noses pink; use marker to outline noses and draw over transferred lines.

5. For handle, cut a $1^1/_2$"w strip from around remaining bottle. Glue a length of ribbon along center of handle. Glue ends of handle to inside of basket at marks. Center buttons on outside of basket over handle ends; mark hole placement. Use

ice pick to punch holes; sew buttons on basket.

6. Tie four 8" lengths of ribbon into bows and glue one below each bunny face.

EASTER PARADE

*T*here's an Easter parade in town and it's coming to your house! This precious goose family is sure to bring spring cheer to your décor while making use of some otherwise useless discards. Lightbulbs, acorns, and paper egg cartons become geese shapes when covered with "recycled" paper pulp. Bright paint and a pretty bonnet dress up Momma Goose, and ribbon bows make the goslings especially sweet.

EGG CARTON AND LIGHTBULB MOMMA GOOSE AND GOSLINGS

MOMMA GOOSE

Recycled items: paper egg cartons, standard lightbulb, and miniature artificial flowers

You will also need tracing paper; utility scissors; ¼" dia. hole punch; hot glue gun; white spray primer; yellow, orange, green, black, and white acrylic paint; paintbrushes; clear acrylic spray sealer; two blue buttons; and ¼"w ribbon.

Allow primer, paint, and sealer to dry after each application.

1. Trace goose patterns, page 153, onto tracing paper; cut out. Use patterns to cut two wings and two feet (one of each in reverse), one tail, and bonnet brim from egg cartons. Referring to Fig. 1, cut egg cups to form base, bonnet, head, and upper and lower bills. Punch six circles from carton.

Fig. 1

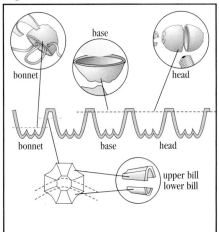

2. Referring to Goose Assembly Diagram, page 140, glue brim to bonnet, head pieces together, and feet pieces together. Glue base, feet, tail, and head to bulb; glue bills to head. Glue circles to bottoms of "toes."

3. Use egg cartons and follow *Paper Making*, page 159, to make paper pulp. Press pulp onto body, sculpting areas around neck and tail; allow to dry.

4. Glue wings to body.

5. Apply primer to goose and bonnet. Paint body yellow, then feet and bill orange; paint bonnet green. Apply two coats of sealer to goose and bonnet.

6. Glue buttons to face for eyes. Paint pupils black with white highlights.

7. Punch a hole in each side of bonnet for ribbon. Glue flowers to bonnet. From inside bonnet, thread ends of a length of ribbon through holes. Place bonnet on goose; bring ribbon ends to front of bonnet and tie into a bow at neck.

GOSLINGS

Recycled items: paper egg cartons, large real or artificial acorns, and small appliance lightbulbs

You will also need tracing paper, utility scissors, $1/4$" dia. hole punch, hot glue gun, white spray primer, yellow and orange acrylic paint, paintbrushes, clear acrylic spray sealer, small black buttons, and $1/4$"w ribbon.

Allow primer, paint, and sealer to dry after each application.

1. Trace gosling patterns, page 153, onto tracing paper; cut out. For each gosling, use patterns to cut two wings and two feet (one of each in reverse), one tail, and upper and lower bills from the flat part of egg cartons. Refer to Fig. 1 to cut a $1/4$" deep section from bottom of one egg cup for base. Punch six circles from carton for supports for bottom of feet.

2. Referring to Gosling Assembly Diagram, page 140, glue feet pieces together. Glue bill pieces to smooth end of acorn for head. Glue base, feet, tail, and head to bulb. Glue circles to bottoms of "toes."

3. Use egg cartons and follow *Paper Making*, page 159, to make paper pulp. Press pulp onto body, sculpting areas around neck and tail; allow to dry.

4. Glue wings to body.

5. Apply primer to gosling. Paint body yellow, then feet and bill orange. Apply two coats of sealer to gosling.

6. Glue buttons to face for eyes.

7. Tie a length of ribbon into a bow around neck.

HEARTFELT CENTERPIECE

For a special bride and groom, make a great keepsake centerpiece! This elegant frame was once little more than a cardboard candy box. After cutting an opening for the picture, you simply decorate the box with crumpled tissue paper and delicate wedding trims. A beautiful floral arrangement at the base includes handmade roses.

HEART CENTERPIECE FRAME

Recycled items: a heart-shaped cardboard candy box with lid, photograph, white and desired color tissue paper (we used peach), decoration for center of bow (we used a satin leaf with a pearl), corrugated cardboard, several white plastic bags, and artificial flowers and leaves

You will also need a craft knife and cutting mat, white spray primer, white spray paint, paintbrush, découpage glue, low-temperature glue gun, decorative trim, wire-edged ribbon, two plastic wedding rings with doves, 9" dia. plastic foam disc, T-pins, assorted lengths of wired floral picks, and green floral tape (if desired).

Use low-temperature glue gun for all gluing unless otherwise indicated.

1. To make a flat bottom for frame, cut 2" from point of lid (frame) and bottom of candy box (frame back). Draw desired shape on front of box lid for opening to fit photograph; cut out.

2. Apply primer, then white paint to frame and frame back; allow to dry.

3. Working in small sections, use paintbrush to apply a thin layer of découpage glue to front of frame, overlapping edges to back and scrunching pieces of tissue paper into glue, cover frame front with white tissue paper and allow to dry.

4. Beginning at bottom, glue lengths of trim along outside and opening edges of frame. Tie ribbon into a bow; glue bow to frame, decoration to center of bow, and rings to frame.

5. For base, cut an 8" x 10" piece of cardboard; cut foam disc in half and discard one half. With curve of foam piece flush with one 10" side of cardboard, center and glue foam to cardboard. Crumple, then smooth peach tissue paper; spot glue paper over entire base.

6. Center and glue bottom of frame to covered cardboard against back of foam on base; secure frame to foam with T-pins, inserting pins through back of frame. Tape photograph behind opening in frame; place frame back on frame.

7. (*Note*: Use picks of varying lengths for roses to create differing heights in arrangement.) For each rose, cut a 7" x 23" strip from one white bag; fold strip in half lengthwise. With fold at top and referring to Fig. 1, fold and wrap strip to make rose center; glue in place. Continue rolling strip around rose center, winding upwards slightly and gluing in place as you go (pushing bag up with your thumb, and spot gluing between layers, helps shape petals). Wrap bottom of rose center with wire from pick; if desired, wrap bottom of rose and wire with floral tape.

Fig. 1

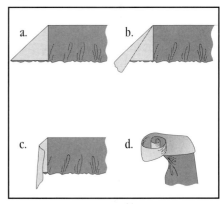

8. Arrange roses and artificial flowers and leaves on base.

Add sizzle to your Fourth of July celebration with a festive caddy that will really get your picnic table organized. Constructed from a cardboard drink carrier, this convenient keeper will tote your disposable dinnerware in patriotic style. Paper towel tubes are easily transformed into "firecrackers" for holding straws, utensils, and an American flag or two!

PATRIOTIC PICNIC CADDY

Recycled items: cardboard drink carrier for four drinks, two paper towel tubes, and lightweight cardboard (we used a cereal box)

You will also need a paring knife, two coordinating fabrics, spray adhesive, craft knife and cutting mat, hot glue gun, metallic party sprays with stars, and rickrack.

1. Using paring knife, carefully disassemble carrier; place on a flat surface. If necessary, refer to Cutting Diagram to cut away fold-up flaps from carrier, creating two new tabs to use for reassembly. Remove drink separator (area in grey) from one side of carrier to accommodate plates.

2. Cut a piece of fabric 1" larger on all sides than unfolded carrier. Place fabric, right side down, on a flat surface. Apply spray adhesive to one side of carrier. Center unfolded carrier, adhesive side down, on fabric; press firmly to secure. Trim fabric even with edges of carrier. Use craft knife to cut out handle holes and cut through drink separator slits.

3. Repeat Step 2 to cover opposite side of carrier.

4. Gluing new tabs to outside bottom of carrier, reassemble carrier.

5. For each "firecracker," cut an 8" piece from paper towel tube. Draw around one end of tube on cardboard; cut out circle and glue to bottom of tube. Cut a 6½" x 9" piece of coordinating fabric. Apply spray adhesive to wrong side of fabric piece; center and smooth around tube. Clip fabric ends and smooth to bottom and inside top of tube. Insert ends of star sprays into tube.

6. Glue rickrack along edges of carrier and around tops of firecrackers. Glue firecrackers to sides of carrier.

CUTTING DIAGRAM

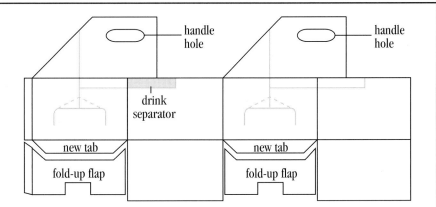

handle hole

handle hole

drink separator

new tab

fold-up flap

new tab

fold-up flap

BRAG BAG

*P*roudly display your favorite faces with our clever "brag bag." Transform ordinary zippered clear vinyl bags into a fashionable tote by adding a vinyl strap and sewing in an extra vinyl piece to create pockets for holding photos. Braided trim and buttons make this fun accessory especially stylish.

PLASTIC TOTE BAG

Recycled items: two clear vinyl bags with zippers, photographs, assorted buttons, and braided trim

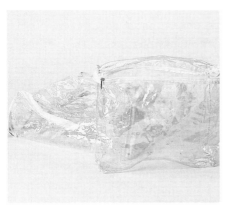

You will also need embroidery floss and a low-temperature glue gun.

1. For tote, measure height and width of one bag front; subtract ¼" from each measurement. Cut a piece of vinyl the determined measurements from remaining bag.

2. Using six strands of floss, sew bottom and sides of vinyl piece to inside front of tote; work additional stitching to form pockets to fit photographs. To insert photographs, carefully cut a slit through one layer of plastic at top of each pocket.

3. Cut a 3"w strip of vinyl the desired length for handle, piecing as necessary. Fold strip into thirds lengthwise; stitch along each long edge. Stitch one end of handle at each side of bag.

4. Use lengths of floss to sew buttons to front of tote; glue trim along top of tote.

"SPOOK-TACULAR" TREAT CANS

*M*ake someone's Halloween *"spook-tacular" with these cute jack-o'-lantern treat cans! It's a snap to cover cardboard snack chip cans with painted paper and then cut the pumpkin's facial features and the whimsical bats from flattened aluminum cans. Twisted pieces of wire become fitting handles, and bright orange raffia adds a haunting touch.*

CARDBOARD TREAT CANS

Recycled items: paper bag, cardboard snack chip cans, and 12-oz. aluminum beverage cans

You will also need white spray primer, orange and black spray paint, craft glue, utility scissors, tracing paper, awl, black craft wire, wire cutters, and orange raffia.

Allow primer, paint, and glue to dry after each application.

1. Cut down seam of bag; cut away and discard bottom. Crumple, then smooth remaining paper piece; spray with primer, then orange paint.

2. For each treat can, measure height and circumference of snack can and add

$^1/_2$" to each measurement; cut a piece of painted paper the determined measurements. Overlapping at back and with extra $^1/_2$" at top of can, glue paper piece to can; glue top edge of paper to inside of can.

3. Cutting through opening in beverage can, cut down can to bottom rim; cut away and discard top and bottom of can. Flatten remaining can piece.

4. Trace patterns, page 154, onto tracing paper; cut out. Use patterns to cut two bats, one of each eye, one nose, and one mouth from can piece.

5. Use awl to punch a hole on each side of can for handle; punch two holes, $^1/_4$" apart, at center of each bat.

6. Apply primer, then black paint to bats, eyes, nose, and mouth.

7. Thread one end of a length of wire through one hole in can; leaving a 4" tail, twist wire around itself to secure. Curl wire tail around a pencil. For handle, form one or two curls in wire; thread one bat onto handle, then add additional curls before threading wire through second hole in can. Leaving a 5" tail, twist wire around itself to secure; curl wire end and add remaining bat.

8. Glue eyes, nose, and mouth on front of can. Tie lengths of raffia into a bow around one end of handle.

COAT HANGER CORNUCOPIA

Spice up your harvest décor with a one-of-a-kind cornucopia. Easily designed from coat hangers and rusted craft wire, it's as economical to make as it is decorative. Fill the finished project with a bounty of fall fruits and vegetables for a beautiful harvest centerpiece to enjoy throughout the fall season.

Recycled items: three dark-colored, lightweight wire coat hangers

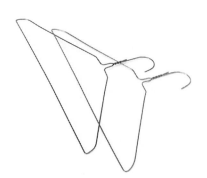

You will also need pliers, new roll of paper towels, wire cutters, and rusted craft wire.

Use pliers to bend wires as necessary.

1. Use pliers to untwist hangers and straighten out. Overlapping ends 2", twist ends of hangers together to form one long piece of wire.

2. Shaping largest spirals first, and gradually decreasing diameter of spirals, bend wire around paper towels to form spirals for cornucopia; twist wire ends around nearest spiral to hold shape.

3. Cut several lengths of craft wire 4" to 6" longer than length of cornucopia. Twisting one end of wire twice around largest spiral to secure in place, working from largest to smallest spiral, and wrapping craft wire around each spiral once, "weave" craft wire between spirals (Fig. 1). Spacing about 1" apart, repeat until cornucopia is rigid.

Fig. 1

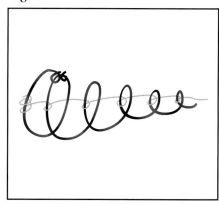

4. Cut several more long lengths of craft wire; working from largest to smallest end, wrap wire around cornucopia, twisting wire around the rusted wire lengths in Step 3.

5. Gather ends of craft wire at tip of cornucopia; wrap another length of craft wire around gathers to secure, then curl craft wire ends.

SNOWY VILLAGE

*B*ring the mood of an old-fashioned holiday to your home with our charming winter village. Constructed using various cartons and cardboard boxes, this appealing project is a wonderful way to get young people involved in creative recycling! A string of lights illuminates each "snow"-sprinkled building, while twig trees and evergreen garlands add realism to the miniature Yuletide town.

WINTER VILLAGE

Recycled items: two 1-qt. and two 1-pint beverage cartons, cardboard soft drink flat or box lid, small box for chimney, corrugated packing cardboard, evergreen garland, twigs for trees and snowman arms, and two small pebbles for eyes

You will also need a craft knife; white spray primer; hot glue gun; gold, tan, beige, dark brown, red, cream, brown, white, and orange acrylic paint; assorted flat paintbrushes; transparent tape; yellow cellophane; miniature Christmas wreath and swag; glitter textured snow medium; 6" of ¹⁄₈" dia. dowel; red bead to fit on end of dowel; white and red card stock; drill and bits; electrical tape; battery-operated miniature light set; large nail; toothpick; polyester batting; and glitter "snow" flakes.

Refer to Painting Techniques, page 156, before beginning project. Allow primer and paint to dry after each application.

1. Open tops of cartons. Referring to Fig. 1, cut sections from carton tops.

Fig. 1

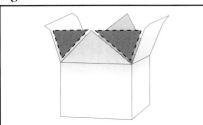

2. Apply primer to soft drink flat, cartons, and box for chimney. Glue quart-size cartons together to form large house. For small houses, paint one pint-size carton gold and one tan. Paint large house beige and chimney dark brown.

3. Draw windows and doors on houses; cut out window openings.

4. Using a flat brush, paint red bricks on large house, cream bricks on tan house, and brown bricks on chimney. Paint window frames, doors, shutters, and other details on houses as desired.

5. Use transparent tape to secure a piece of cellophane behind each window.

6. Referring to Fig. 2, glue tops of cartons closed to form gabled roof or side of house.

Fig. 2

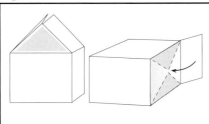

7. For roofs, cut two 3" x 7" pieces of cardboard for large house, two 3" x 4" pieces for gold house, two 2¹⁄₂" x 4³⁄₄" pieces for tan house, and a 1¹⁄₄" x 2" piece for awning; glue to houses.

8. For chimney, cut flaps from ends of box. Referring to Fig. 3, hold box next to roof and mark cutting lines; cut out notch along marked lines. Use cut-out piece to mark cutting lines on opposite side of box; cut out notch. Cut chimney to desired height; glue on roof. Glue wreath and swag to houses.

Fig. 3

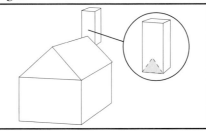

9. For base, place soft drink flat bottom side up; glue houses to base. Paint walkways, then apply snow medium to base; allow to dry.

10. For signpost, paint dowel white, then paint a red spiral stripe around post. Glue bead to top of post.

11. Photocopy sign designs, page 152, onto white card stock; cut out. Glue signs to red card stock; cut out. Glue signs to post.

12. For each evergreen, remove a sprig from garland and wrap around a pencil to form tree shape.

13. Referring to Fig. 4, drill holes through bottom of base under houses for lights. Use electrical tape to secure lights in holes on underside of base.

Fig. 4

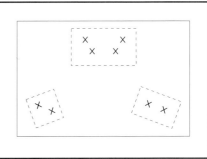

14. Use nail to punch holes through top of base for trees and signpost. Use glue to secure trees and signpost in holes.

15. For snowman nose, paint end of toothpick orange; cut ¹⁄₂" from painted end of toothpick. Use snow medium to form snowman on base; decorate snowman with eyes, nose, and arms before medium dries.

16. Arrange and glue batting around base.

17. Apply snow medium to trees, signpost, rooftops, awning, chimney, and batting; sprinkle glitter flakes over wet snow medium and allow to dry.

Shimmering "Foil" Tree

*N*o one will ever guess that the branches of this shimmering Christmas tree are really pieces of burnt brown paper bags! A simple technique of heating glue-coated paper over a candle flame produces the look of foil on the branches. When the leaves are glued to a plastic cone perched on a dowel anchored in a decorated cardboard can, the result is a crafty tree with lots of sparkle and shine.

BURNT BAG TREE

Recycled items: lightweight cardboard, brown paper bags, and a 9-oz. cardboard nut can

You will also need tracing paper, craft glue, candle, 12"h x ³/₄" dia. dowel, black acrylic paint, paintbrush, silver metallic buffing compound, plaster of paris, hot glue gun, 12" tall x 4" dia. plastic foam cone, and grey Spanish moss.

Caution: Use extreme caution when working with an open flame.

Use craft glue for all gluing unless otherwise indicated. Allow glue and paint to dry after each application.

1. Trace leaf and topper patterns, page 152, onto tracing paper; cut out, then glue to a piece of cardboard and cut out. Use leaf pattern to cut out enough leaves from brown bags to cover plastic cone; use topper pattern to cut out one topper from brown bags.

2. To cover base, measure height of can between rims, then measure circumference of can and add ¹/₂"; cut a piece from brown bag the determined measurements. Overlapping at back, glue piece around can.

3. Working in small sections on one leaf at a time, apply an uneven layer of glue to one side of leaf. Hold glue side of leaf just above a candle flame and slowly move over flame until glue turns a silver-black color. (*Note*: If leaf catches on fire, gently blow out flame and continue heating glue.) Repeat step to burn topper and base. Allow leaves, topper, and base to cool.

4. For tree trunk, insert one end of dowel 5" into center of large end of cone. Paint trunk black.

5. Following buffing compound manufacturer's directions, apply buffing compound over burnt areas on leaves, topper, trunk, and base.

6. Follow plaster manufacturer's instructions to mix enough plaster to almost fill base; pour into base and allow to slightly harden. Insert trunk into base; allow plaster to harden.

7. Starting at bottom of cone, slightly bending leaves vertically along center, and overlapping tiers, hot glue leaves in tiers around cone. Overlapping ends at back, hot glue topper to top of cone.

8. Glue moss to top of base.

GLIMMERY GIFT TOTES

Why not present your special offerings in bags that are nice enough to be gifts themselves? Ordinary brown paper bags are transformed into glimmering gift totes when you découpage them with torn pieces of crumpled tissue paper and dry brush with metallic paint. Luminescent wired ribbon creates gorgeous bows, and shiny twisted wire trim provides both functional and decorative handles.

DÉCOUPAGED GIFT BAGS

Recycled items: white tissue paper and paper bags (we used a lunch-size bag and a small grocery bag)

You will also need découpage glue, foam brush, gold and silver acrylic paint, paintbrushes, wired ribbon, hot glue gun, wire cutters, and wired trim.

Allow paint to dry after each application. Use découpage glue for all gluing unless otherwise indicated.

1. For each bag, tear tissue paper into small pieces. Working in small sections and overlapping pieces, apply glue to bag, then press and scrunch pieces of tissue

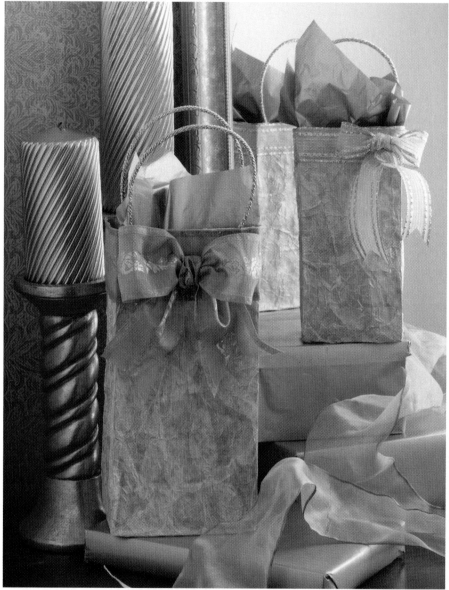

paper into glue, covering outside of bag completely and overlapping slightly to inside; allow to dry. Apply a layer of glue over covered part of bag to seal and allow to dry.

2. *Dry Brush*, page 157, bag with paint. (We used gold paint on our large bag, and silver and gold for the stripes on our smaller bag.)

3. Overlapping at front of bag, glue a length of ribbon along top edge of bag. Tie another length of ribbon into a bow; hot glue knot to ribbon on front of bag.

4. For handles, hot glue lengths of trim at inside top of bag.

CRAFTY GREETINGS

*M*ake *your holiday greetings distinctive with "new" cards, tags, and bookmarks that you create using art and verses cut from old greeting cards! Just start with a blank card or a piece of folded card stock and embellish as you please. Use markers and colored pencils to add borders for one-of-a-kind greetings with your personal touch.*

CARDS, BOOKMARKS, AND TAGS FROM OLD CARDS

Recycled items: old greeting cards

You will also need a craft glue stick, purchased blank cards and envelopes (or card stock cut and folded to fit envelopes), card stock for bookmarks and tags, fine-point markers, colored pencils, raffia, ¹/₈"w ribbon, hot glue gun, and a ¹/₄" dia. hole punch.

Use craft glue stick for all gluing unless otherwise indicated.

1. Cut desired pictures, designs, or shapes from old cards.

2. For each new card or envelope, glue cutout(s) to front of blank card (we left a ¹/₂" to ³/₄" plain border) and envelope. Cut a sentiment from an old card and glue inside new card.

3. Cut card stock desired size for each bookmark or tag. Glue cutout(s) to bookmark or tags as desired.

4. Use markers to draw borders around cutouts and colored pencils to color any details. Tie raffia and ribbon into small bows; hot glue to cards, bookmarks, or tags as desired.

5. If making bookmarks, punch a hole at top center of each bookmark. Fold a 10" length of ribbon in half; insert loop through hole, then wrap ends around top of bookmark and thread through loop.

HEAVENLY ANGEL PIN

*S*how a special "angel" how heavenly she is with this delightful fashion pin! Crafted using salvaged jewelry pieces in a variety of shapes, this adorable brooch is a spirited gift idea for someone dear!

JEWELRY ANGEL PIN

Recycled items: pieces of jewelry in shapes to form angel body, head, wings, halo, and adornments

You will also need wire cutters, jumbo craft stick, household cement, and a pin back.

Use wire cutters to cut pieces from jewelry to fit on pin as desired. Use household cement for all gluing; allow to dry after each application.

1. Arrange pieces of jewelry to form angel (such as arranging heart earrings for wings behind an oval brooch for head).

2. Cut craft stick to fit length of angel.

3. Glue angel pieces to craft stick; add adornments to complete angel.

4. Glue pin back to back of angel.

BEJEWELED ORNAMENTS

*R*ound up those bits of broken jewelry and random buttons to make these easy and kid-friendly ornaments! Just create your own designs as you glue chains, charms, jewels, buttons, and beads to pieces of painted cardboard cut from a cereal box. These tree trimmers make great projects for children and adults alike!

JEWELRY ORNAMENTS

Recycled items: cardboard (we used a cereal box), necklace or bracelet chains, and items to decorate ornaments (we used jewelry, charms, buttons, beads, and jewels)

You will also need tracing paper, acrylic paint, paintbrush, wire cutters, and household cement.

Use wire cutters to cut chains and pieces from jewelry to fit on ornament as desired. Use household cement for all gluing; allow to dry after each application.

1. Trace desired pattern, page 154, onto tracing paper; cut out. Use pattern to cut ornament backing from cardboard.

2. Paint backing; allow to dry.

3. Glue chain along edges of ornament. Glue ends of a length of chain at top back of ornament for hanger.

4. Arrange and glue jewelry pieces on backing to complete ornament.

135

SWEET SNOWMAN

W̲ho would guess that a collection of plastic disposables could become a whimsical treat bag? This snowman is crafted from a detergent bottle lid, a juice bottle, and a piece of bubble wrap gathered around a handful of goodies. Dressed up with fabric strips and berries, this oh-so-charming fellow is sure to be a hit at your holiday party!

SNOWMAN GOODY BAG

Recycled items: a small clear plastic beverage bottle, plastic bubble wrap, twist tie, liquid laundry detergent lid, and fabric scraps

You will also need utility scissors, ice pick, small treats or candies (we used candy-coated pretzels), 12" length of black plastic-coated craft wire, craft saw, hot glue gun, artificial miniature greenery sprig with red berries, and black and orange permanent fine-point markers.

1. For snowman head, use utility scissors to cut top 3" from bottle; discard bottom of bottle. Use ice pick to punch one hole 1/2" from cut edge on each side of head for armholes.

2. For body, cut a 10" dia. circle from bubble wrap. Place circle, bubble side down, on a flat surface. Place candies at center of circle, then gather edges over candies; use twist tie to secure gathers.

3. For arms, wrap center of wire twice around gathers on body, thread ends of wire through armholes and pull taut. Bend ends of wire to form fingers.

4. For hat, use craft saw to cut away bottom of lid just under rim. Covering threads on head, glue hat to top of head. Knot a strip of fabric around hat for hatband; glue greenery to hatband.

5. Use markers to draw black eyes, eyebrows, and mouth and an orange nose on head. Tie a strip of fabric around snowman for scarf.

PLAYFUL SNOWMEN

*S*end the kids on a scavenger hunt for loose game pieces and use their finds to make these playful snowman ornaments! Both rectangular and round pieces become cute frosty fellows with a bit of paint and simple craft supplies. These winsome creations look great on your own tree and also make fun little presents.

SNOWMAN ORNAMENTS

Recycled items: wooden game pieces, craft sticks, artificial holly sprigs with berries, and ¹/₂" x 10" torn fabric scrap pieces

You will also need a drill and small bit; white spray primer; white, black, red, pink, and orange acrylic paint; paintbrushes; utility scissors; craft glue; black permanent fine-point marker; and 6" lengths of craft wire.

Allow primer, glue, and paint to dry after each application.

1. For each ornament, drill a hole through top of game piece. Apply primer, then white paint to game piece.

2. For rectangle ornament, paint top of ornament black for hat; cut a piece of craft stick 1" wider than game piece, paint black, and glue in place for hat brim. Glue holly sprig to hat.

3. For round ornament, paint a red stocking cap at top of ornament; use marker to draw brim on hat.

4. Paint black *Dots*, page 157, for eyes and mouths on ornaments; paint white dots for highlights in eyes on round

ornaments. Paint orange noses on ornaments; use fingertip to paint pink cheeks. Use marker to outline noses, and to add eyebrows to round ornaments.

5. For hanger, thread one wire length through hole in ornament and twist ends to secure. For scarf, fray ends of fabric strip, then tie around rectangle snowman.

PATTERNS

BIG LIGHTBULB BUG
(page 27)

ASSEMBLY DIAGRAM

STACKED SPOOLS CANDLESTICKS
(page 59)

ASSEMBLY DIAGRAM

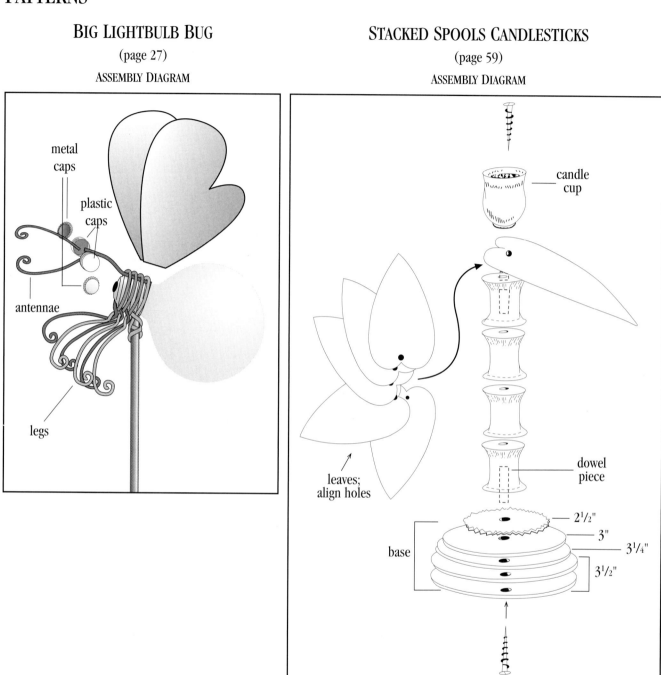

metal caps

plastic caps

antennae

legs

candle cup

leaves; align holes

dowel piece

base

$2^1/_2$"

3"

$3^1/_4$"

$3^1/_2$"

EGYPTIAN SAFETY PIN BROOCH

(page 81)

ASSEMBLY DIAGRAM

one half of pin

SHUTTER AND MAILING TUBES TABLE

(page 101)

ASSEMBLY DIAGRAM

BROOCH WITH CURLS

(page 81)

ASSEMBLY DIAGRAM

STARBURST BUTTONS BROOCH

(page 81)

FIG. 1

FIG. 2

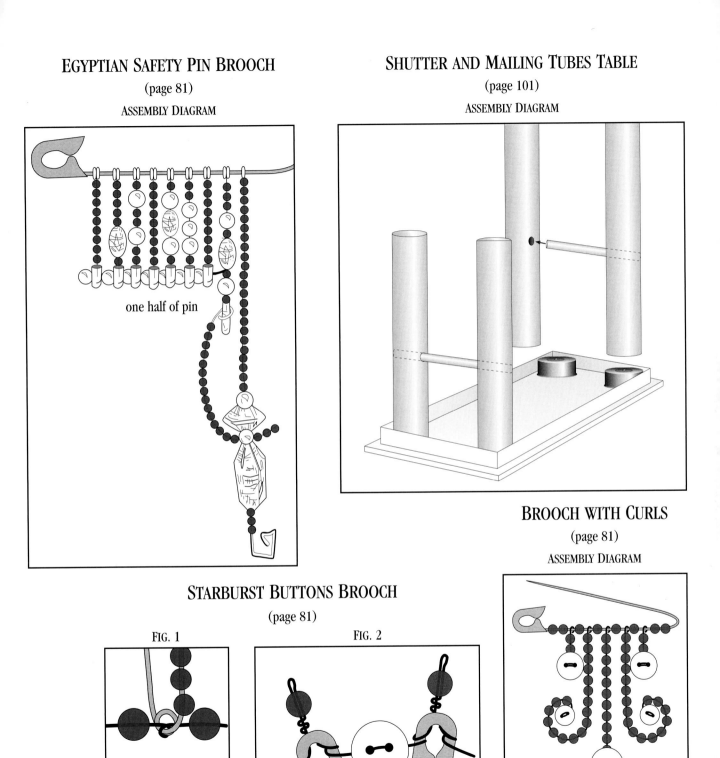

PATTERNS (continued)

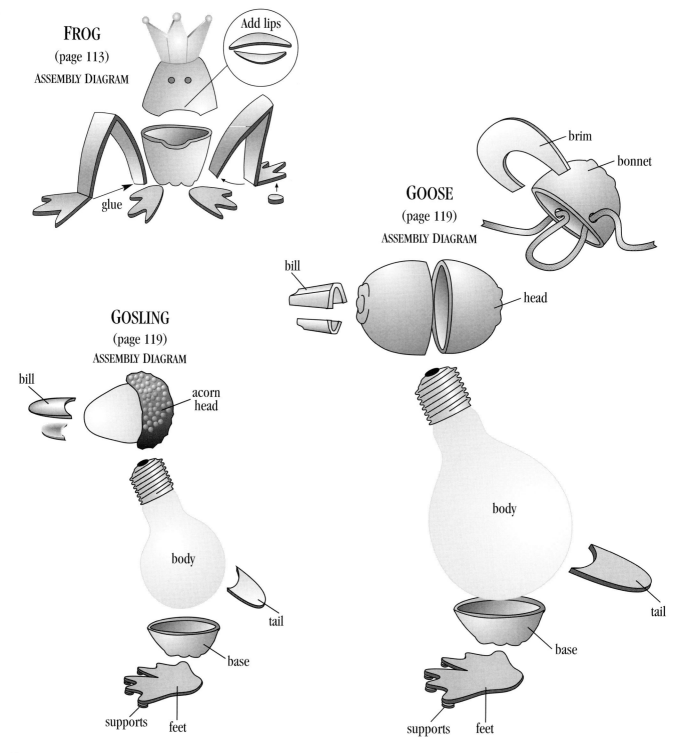

FROG
(page 113)

ASSEMBLY DIAGRAM

Add lips

glue

GOOSE
(page 119)

ASSEMBLY DIAGRAM

brim

bonnet

bill

head

GOSLING
(page 119)

ASSEMBLY DIAGRAM

bill

acorn head

body

tail

base

supports   feet

body

tail

base

supports   feet

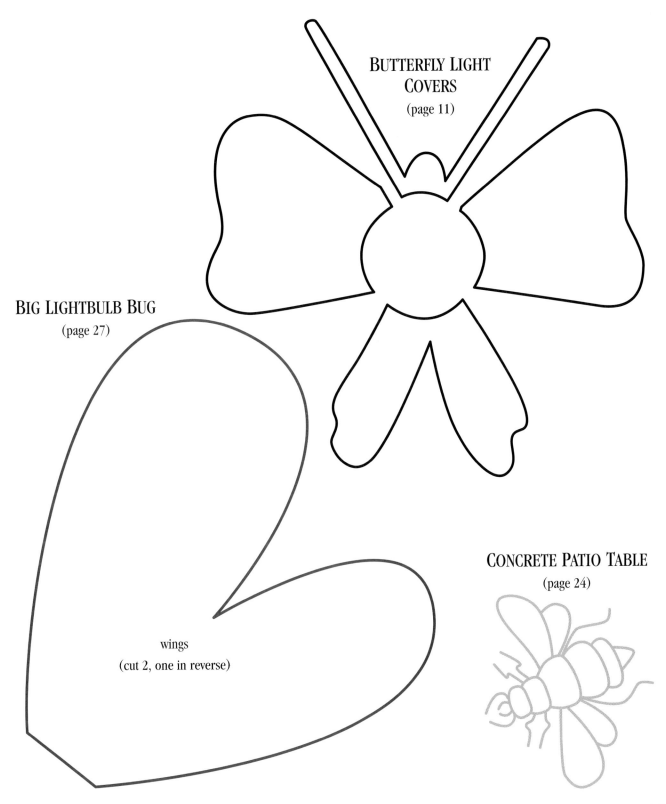

BUTTERFLY LIGHT
COVERS
(page 11)

BIG LIGHTBULB BUG
(page 27)

wings
(cut 2, one in reverse)

CONCRETE PATIO TABLE
(page 24)

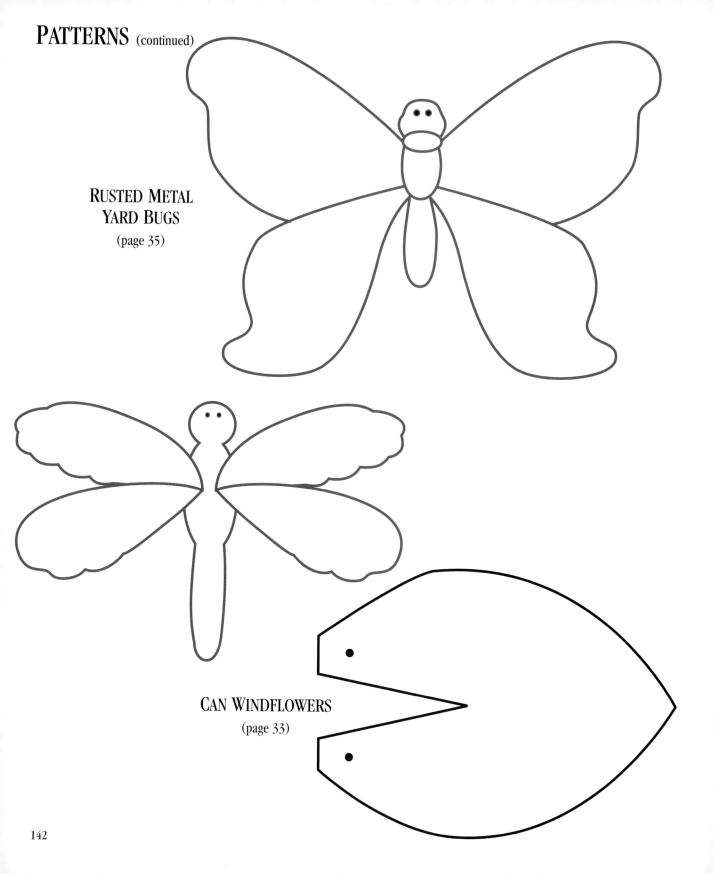

PATTERNS (continued)

RUSTED METAL
YARD BUGS
(page 35)

CAN WINDFLOWERS
(page 33)

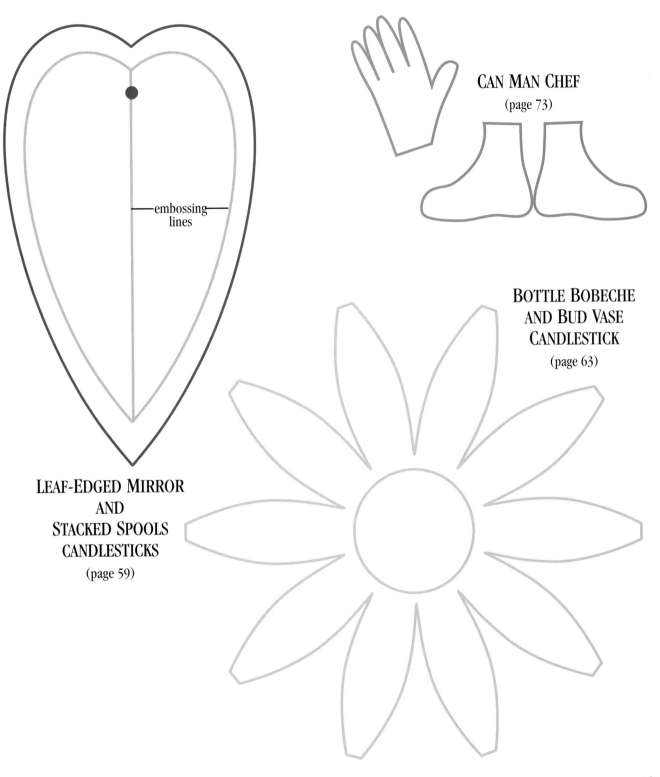

embossing
lines

CAN MAN CHEF
(page 73)

BOTTLE BOBECHE
AND BUD VASE
CANDLESTICK
(page 63)

LEAF-EDGED MIRROR
AND
STACKED SPOOLS
CANDLESTICKS
(page 59)

PATTERNS (continued)

STICK FRAME WITH EMBOSSED
ALUMINUM LEAVES
(page 53)

VINYL CALICO CAT MAT
(page 67)

1 square = 2"

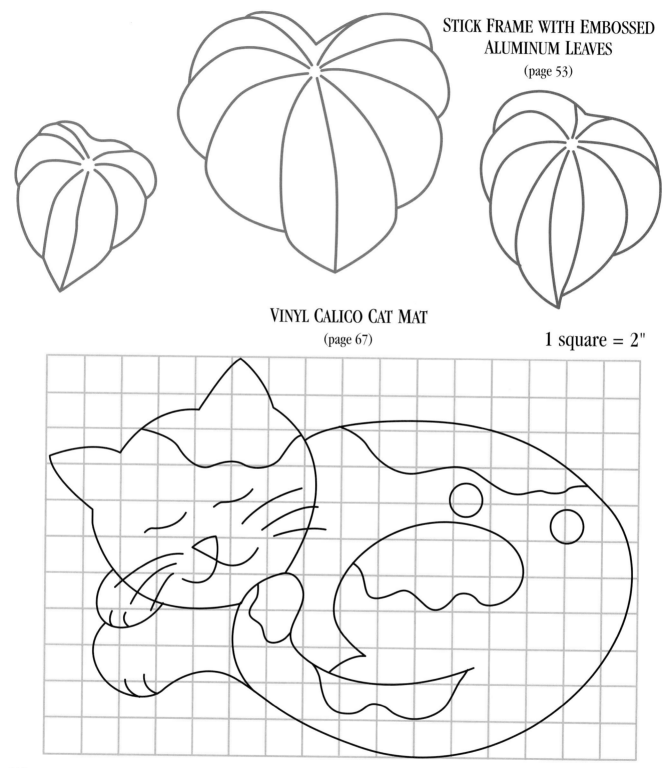

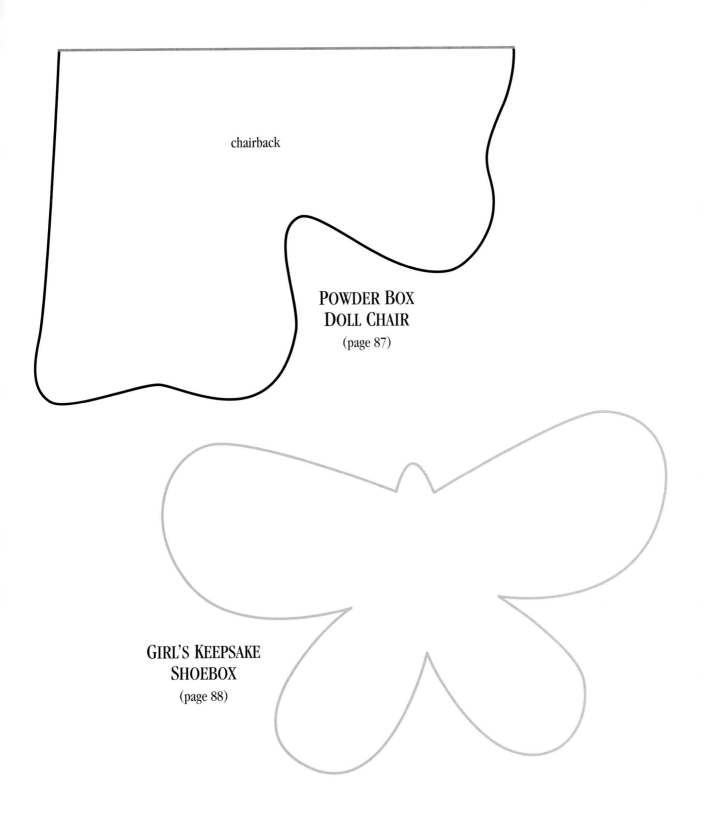

chairback

**POWDER BOX
DOLL CHAIR**
(page 87)

**GIRL'S KEEPSAKE
SHOEBOX**
(page 88)

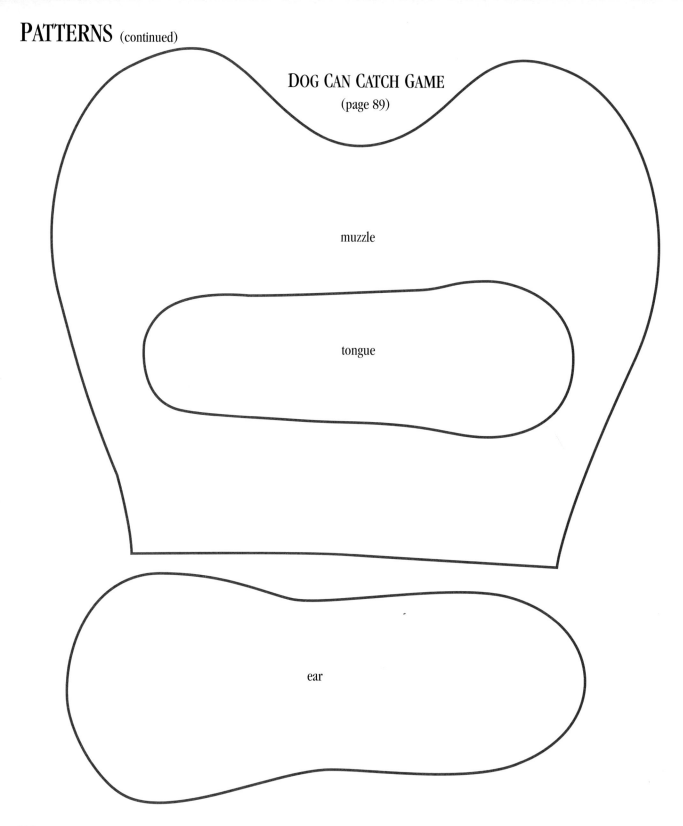

DOG CAN CATCH GAME
(page 89)

muzzle

tongue

ear

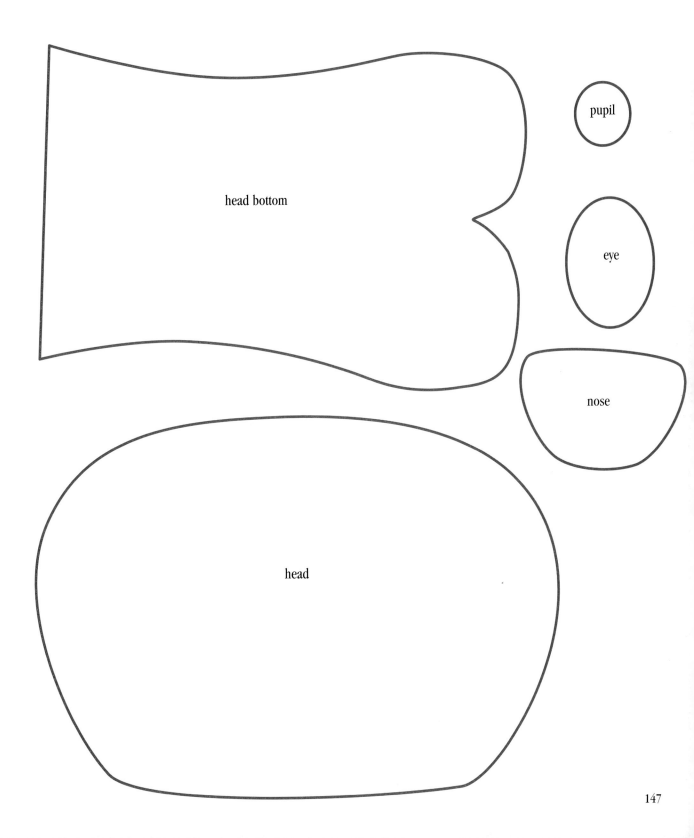

pupil

head bottom

eye

nose

head

PATTERNS (continued)

KID'S HANDS MAGNETS
(page 106)

FRAMED MOSAIC CARD SET
(page 90)

TIN BOX PARTY FAVOR
(page 108)

VALENTINE FAVORS
(page111)

CARTON BABY BLOCK
CENTERPIECE
(page 104)

149

PARTY TREAT CANS
(page 107)

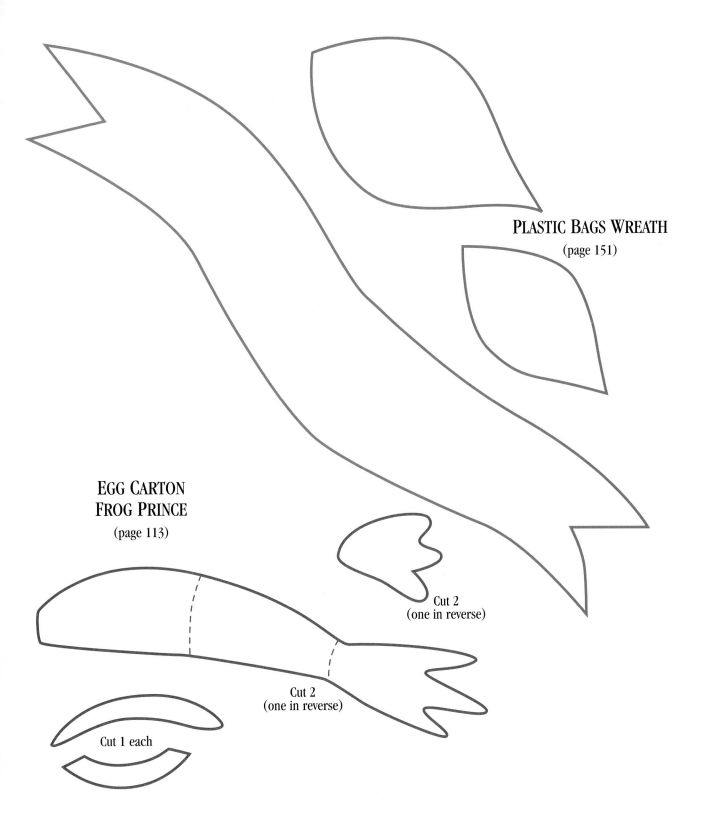

PLASTIC BAGS WREATH
(page 151)

EGG CARTON
FROG PRINCE
(page 113)

Cut 2
(one in reverse)

Cut 2
(one in reverse)

Cut 1 each

PATTERNS (continued)

BLEACH BOTTLE BUNNY BASKET
(page 117)

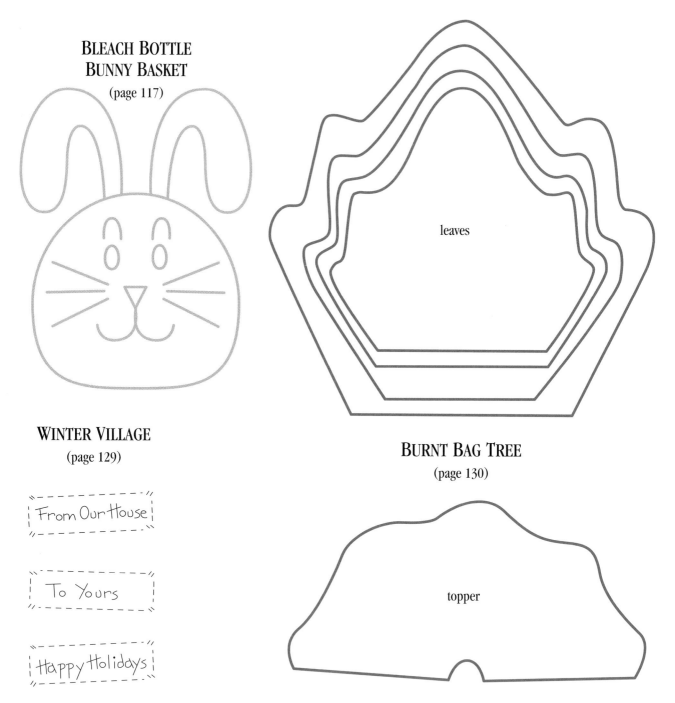

leaves

WINTER VILLAGE
(page 129)

From Our House

To Yours

Happy Holidays

BURNT BAG TREE
(page 130)

topper

Egg Carton and Lightbulb Momma Goose and Goslings

(page 119)

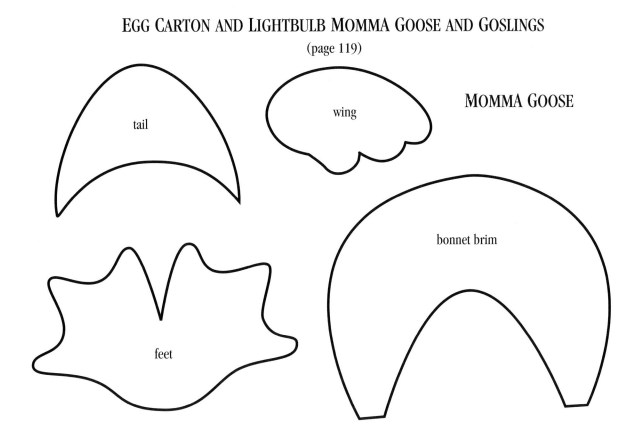

MOMMA GOOSE

tail

wing

bonnet brim

feet

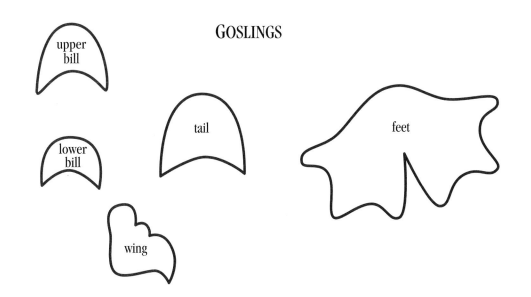

GOSLINGS

upper bill

lower bill

wing

tail

feet

PATTERNS (continued)

CARDBOARD
TREAT CANS

(page 125)

JEWELRY ORNAMENTS

(page 135)

VINYL SERVING MAT

(page 91)

GENERAL INSTRUCTIONS

ADHESIVES

When using any adhesive, carefully follow the manufacturer's instructions.

White craft glue: Recommended for paper. Dry flat.

Tacky craft glue: Recommended for paper, fabric, florals, or wood. Dry flat or secure items with clothespins or straight pins until glue is dry.

Craft glue stick: Recommended for paper or for gluing small, lightweight items to paper or other surfaces. Dry flat.

Fabric glue: Recommended for fabric or paper. Dry flat or secure items with clothespins or straight pins until glue is dry.

Découpage glue: Recommended for découpaging fabric or paper to a surface such as wood or glass. Use purchased découpage glue or mix one part craft glue with one part water.

Hot or low-temperature glue gun: Recommended for paper, fabric, florals, or wood. Hold in place until set.

Spray adhesive: Recommended for paper or fabric. Can be repositioned or permanent. Dry flat.

Household cement: Recommended for ceramic or metal. Secure items with clothespins until glue is dry.

Wood glue: Recommended for wood. Nail, screw, or clamp items together until glue is dry.

Silicone adhesive: Recommended for ceramic, glass, leather, rubber, wood, and plastics. Forms a flexible and waterproof bond.

PAINTING TECHNIQUES

A disposable foam plate makes a good palette for holding and mixing paint colors. It can easily be placed in a large resealable plastic bag to keep remaining paint wet while waiting for an area of applied paint to dry.

As well, when waiting for large areas to dry, before applying a second coat, wrap your paintbrush in plastic wrap and place in the refrigerator to keep paint from drying on your brush. Always clean brushes thoroughly after use to keep them in good condition.

TRANSFERRING A PATTERN

Trace pattern onto tracing paper. Place transfer paper, coated side down, between project and traced pattern. Use removable tape to secure pattern to project. Use a pencil to transfer outlines of design to project (press lightly to avoid smudges and heavy lines that are difficult to cover). If necessary, use a soft eraser to remove any smudges.

TRANSFERRING DETAILS

To transfer detail lines to design, position pattern and transfer paper over painted basecoat and use a pencil to lightly transfer detail lines onto project.

ADDING DETAILS

Use a permanent marker or paint pen (usually with a fine-tip) to draw over transferred detail lines or to create freehanded details on project.

PAINTING BASECOATS

A basecoat is a solid color of paint that covers the project's entire surface.

Use a medium round brush for large areas and a small round brush for small areas. Do not overload brush. Allowing to dry between coats, apply several thin coats of paint to project.

AGED FINISHES

This technique creates a faux-aged finish.

Allowing to dry between applications, paint project the desired basecoat color. Randomly apply a thin layer of floor paste wax with a soft cloth, or rub a candle over areas on project to be aged (such as the edges). Paint project the desired top coat color and allow to dry. Lightly sand project to remove some of the paint for a gently-aged look. Wipe project with a tack cloth to remove dust, then seal with clear acrylic sealer.

"C" STROKE

Dip an angle or flat paintbrush in paint. Touch tip to surface, pulling brush to the left. Pull brush toward you while applying pressure. When stroke is desired length, lift brush gradually while pulling to the right to form the tail of the stroke.

COLOR WASH

A color wash is a light coloration of a project surface. It is similar to Dry Brush, yet creates a softer look that penetrates the project's surface.

To create a color wash, mix one part acrylic paint with two to three parts water. Dip paintbrush in color wash and brush across the area to receive color. Decrease pressure on the brush as you move outward. Repeat to create desired effect.

DOTS

Dip handle end of paintbrush for larger dots or the end of a toothpick for smaller dots, into paint; touch to painting surface and lift straight up. Dip tip into paint frequently to maintain uniform dots.

DRY BRUSH

This technique creates a random top coat coloration of a project surface. It is similar to a Color Wash, yet creates an aged look that sits on top of the project's surface.

Do not dip brush in water. Dip a stipple brush or old paintbrush in paint; wipe most of the paint off onto a dry paper towel. Lightly rub the brush across the area to receive color. Decrease pressure on the brush as you move outward. Repeat as needed to create the desired coverage of color.

RUSTING

This technique creates a faux-rusted finish on project's surface.

1. Spray surface of project with a rusty-red color primer.

2. For paints, unevenly mix one part water to one part orange acrylic paint; unevenly mix one part water to one part dark orange acrylic paint.

3. (*Note*: To create a more natural rusted look, use a paper towel or a clean damp sponge piece to dab off paint in some areas after applying paint. Also, drip a few drops of water onto painted surface while paint is still wet, let them run, and then allow to dry.) Dip a dampened sponge into paint; blot on paper towel to remove excess paint. Allowing to dry after each coat, use a light stamping motion to paint project with orange, then dark orange paint mixtures. Apply sealer to project and allow to dry.

SPATTER PAINTING

This technique creates a speckled look on project's surface.

Dip the bristle tips of a dry toothbrush into paint, blot on a paper towel to remove excess, then pull thumb across bristles to spatter paint on project.

SPONGE PAINTING

This technique creates a soft, mottled look on project's surface.

1. Dampen sponge with water.

2. Dip dampened sponge into paint; blot on paper towel to remove excess paint.

3. Use a light stamping motion to paint project. Allow to dry.

4. If using more than one color of paint, repeat Steps 1 – 3, using a fresh sponge piece for each color.

5. If desired, repeat technique using one color again over areas of other colors, to soften edges or to lighten up a heavy application of one color.

STENCILING

These instructions are written for multicolor stencils. For single-color stencils, make one stencil for the entire design.

1. For first stencil, cut a piece from stencil plastic 1" larger than entire pattern. Center plastic over pattern and use a permanent pen to trace outlines of all areas of first color in stencil cutting key. For placement guidelines, outline remaining colored area using dashed lines. Using a new piece of plastic for each additional color in stencil cutting key, repeat for remaining stencils.

2. Place each plastic piece on cutting mat and use a craft knife to cut out stencil along solid lines, making sure edges are smooth.

3. Hold or tape stencil in place. Using a clean, dry stencil brush or sponge piece, dip brush or sponge in paint. Remove excess paint on a paper towel. Brush or sponge should be almost dry to produce best results. Beginning at edge of cutout area, apply paint in a stamping motion over stencil. If desired, highlight or shade design by stamping a lighter or darker shade of paint in cutout area. Repeat until all areas of first stencil have been painted. Carefully remove stencil and allow paint to dry.

4. Using stencils in order indicated in color key and matching guidelines on stencils to previously stenciled area, repeat Step 3 for remaining stencils.

MAKING PATTERNS

For a more durable pattern, use a permanent pen to trace pattern onto stencil plastic instead of tracing paper. Or cut out the tracing paper pattern, place it on cardboard, draw around it, and then cut out a cardboard pattern.

Place tracing paper over pattern and trace lines of pattern; cut out.

When only a half pattern is shown (indicated by a solid blue line on pattern), fold tracing paper in half. Place the fold along solid blue line and trace pattern half. Turn paper over and draw along pattern half. Open tracing paper and cut out whole pattern.

GENERAL INSTRUCTIONS (continued)

DÉCOUPAGE

1. Cut desired motifs from fabric or paper.

2. Apply découpage glue to wrong sides of motifs.

3. Arrange motifs on project as desired, overlapping as necessary. Smooth in place and allow to dry.

4. Allowing to dry after each application, apply two to three coats of sealer to project.

WORKING WITH WAX

MELTING WAX

Caution: Do not melt wax over an open flame or in a pan placed directly on burner.

1. Cover work area with newspaper.

2. Heat 1" of water in a saucepan to boiling. Add water as necessary.

3. Place wax in a large can. If pouring wax, pinch top rim of can to form a spout. If dipping candles, use a can 2" taller than height of candle to be dipped.

4. To melt wax, place can in boiling water and reduce heat to simmer. If color is desired, melt pieces of crayon or bits of wax color blocks in wax. Use a craft stick to stir, if necessary.

SETTING WICKS

1. Cut a length of wax-coated wick 1" longer than depth of candle container.

2. Using an oven mitt, carefully pour wax into container.

3. Allow wax to harden slightly and insert wick at center of candle. Allow wax to harden completely.

EMBROIDERY STITCHES

BACKSTITCH

Bring needle up at 1; go down at 2. Bring needle up at 3 and back down at 1 (Fig. 1). Continue working to make a continuous line of stitches.

Fig. 1

BLIND STITCH

Come up at 1. Go down at 2 and come up at 3 (Fig. 2). Length of stitches may be varied as desired.

Fig. 2

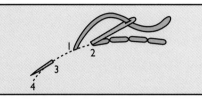

FRENCH KNOT

Bring needle up at 1. Wrap floss once around needle and insert needle at 2, holding floss with non-stitching fingers (Fig. 3). Tighten knot as close to fabric as possible while pulling needle back through fabric. For larger knot, use more strands of floss; wrap only once.

Fig. 3

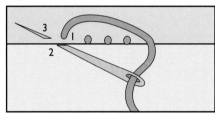

RUNNING STITCH

Make a series of straight stitches with stitch length equal to the space between stitches (Fig. 4).

Fig. 4

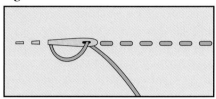

STRAIGHT STITCH

Bring needle up at 1 and go down at 2 (Fig. 5). Length of stitches may be varied as desired.

Fig. 5

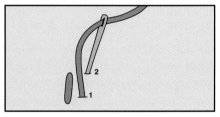

WHIPSTITCH

Referring to Fig. 6, bring needle up at 1; take thread around edge of fabric and bring needle up at 2. Continue stitching along edge of fabric.

Fig. 6

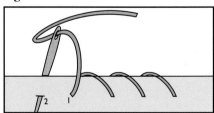

158

COFFEE OR TEA DYEING

Coffee Dyeing: Dissolve two tablespoons instant coffee in two cups water; allow to cool.

Tea Dyeing: Steep one tea bag in two cups hot water; remove bag and allow to cool.

For Both: Immerse fabric in coffee or tea. Soak until desired color is achieved, then stir $\frac{1}{4}$ cup white vinegar into dye water to set color. Remove fabric, rinse, and allow to dry; press if needed.

PAPER MAKING

1. Tear paper to be recycled into pieces about $\frac{1}{2}$" square; place in bucket. Fill bucket with hot water and soak for at least one hour.

2. Wearing rubber gloves, squeeze excess water from a small handful of pre-soaked paper pieces and place in blender; cover with water until blender is half full. Blend at low speed for fifteen seconds, increasing speed to medium, then high, at fifteen second intervals; decrease speed in the same manner. When pulp is no longer lumpy, pour it into a second bucket.

3. With one handful of soaked paper pieces at a time, repeat the blending process until all pieces have been processed.

4. Lay a towel on a flat surface and cover with a piece of screen wire. Scoop pulp from bucket and press onto screen; place another piece of screen, then another towel on pulp and press to let towels absorb excess water. Use prepared pulp to complete project.

FUSIBLE APPLIQUÉS

To prevent darker fabrics from showing through, white or light-colored fabrics may need to be lined with fusible interfacing before applying paper-backed fusible web.

Follow all steps for each appliqué. When tracing patterns for more than one appliqué, leave at least 1" between shapes on web.

To make a reverse appliqué piece, trace pattern onto tracing paper; turn traced pattern over and continue to follow all steps using reversed pattern.

When an appliqué pattern contains shaded areas, trace along entire outer line for appliqué indicated in project instructions. Trace outer lines of shaded areas separately for additional appliqués indicated in project instructions.

Appliqués can be temporarily held in place by touching appliqués with tip of iron. If appliqués are not in desired position, lift and reposition.

1. Use a pencil to trace pattern onto paper side of web as many times as indicated in project instructions for a single fabric. Repeat for additional patterns and fabrics.

2. Follow manufacturer's instructions to fuse traced patterns to wrong side of fabrics. Do not remove paper backing.

3. Cut out appliqué pieces along traced lines. Remove paper backing.

4. Overlapping as necessary, arrange appliqués web side down on project.

5. Fuse appliqués in place.

MACHINE APPLIQUÉ

Unless otherwise indicated in project instructions, set sewing machine for a medium-width zigzag stitch with a short stitch length. When using nylon or metallic thread, use regular thread in bobbin.

1. Pin or baste a piece of stabilizer slightly larger than design to wrong side of background fabric under design.

2. Beginning on straight edge of appliqué if possible, position project under presser foot so that most of stitching will be on appliqué piece. Hold upper thread toward you and sew two or three stitches over thread to prevent raveling. Stitch over all exposed raw edges of appliqué and along detail lines as indicated in project instructions.

3. When stitching is complete, remove stabilizer. Pull loose threads to wrong side of fabric; knot and trim ends.

HAND APPLIQUÉ

1. Leaving $\frac{1}{2}$" between shapes, draw around patterns on right side of fabric.

2. Cut out shapes $\frac{1}{4}$" outside drawn lines. Press edges of shapes $\frac{1}{4}$" to wrong side. Clip curves and points up to, but not through drawn lines. Arrange and pin appliqués on project.

3. Use Blind Stitches to sew edges of appliqués to project.

CREDITS

We want to extend a warm *thank you* to the generous people who allowed us to photograph our projects at their homes: Sandra Cook, Ellison Poe, Duncan and Nancy Porter.

We especially want to thank photographer Jerry R. Davis of Jerry Davis Photography, Little Rock, Arkansas, for his time, patience, and excellent work.